Anxiety & Tension

D0493958

Symptoms, causes, orthodox treatment and
how herbal medicine will help.

Other published and forthcoming titles
in the series include:

IBS & Colitis

Menopause

Migraine & Headaches

Asthma & Bronchitis

Arthritis & Rheumatism

Anxiety & Tension

Jill Wright MNIMH

HERBAL HEALTH

Published in 2002 by
How To Books Ltd, 3 Newtec Place,
Magdalen Road, Oxford OX4 1RE, United Kingdom
Tel: (01865) 793806   Fax: (01865) 248780
email: info@howtobooks.co.uk
www.howtobooks.co.uk

British Library Cataloguing in Publication Data
A catalogue record for this book is available from
the British Library

Edited by Diana Brueton
Cover design by Shireen Nathoo Design, London
Produced for How To Books by Deer Park Productions
Designed and typeset by Shireen Nathoo Design, London
Printed and bound in Great Britain by Bell & Bain Ltd,
Glasgow

Note: The material contained in this book is set out in good
faith for general guidance and no liability can be accepted for
loss or expense incurred as a result of relying in particular
circumstances on statements made in the book. The laws and
regulations are complex and liable to change, and readers
should check the current position with the relevant authorities
before making personal arrangements.

Herbal Health *is an imprint of*
How To Books

Contents

Preface

We hear a lot about stress these days, but how do you know if your anxiety and tension levels are serious enough to need treatment? Serious stress can cause:

- A permanent feeling of butterflies in the stomach.
- Worry about everything.
- Jumping at sudden noises or movements.

High levels of anxiety can make you be easily moved to tears, inclined to tension, prevent you from sleeping well at night and give you nightmares, or have upsetting thoughts during the day.

Is your concentration failing? Do you struggle to find words or remember things you have to do? This may also be due to **anxiety** and **tension**.

Anxiety can cause a wide variety of **physical symptoms**, including pains in the chest, frequent bowel movement, constipation, tendency to strain muscles, headaches, indigestion, skin problems including psoriasis, eczema and even acne, cold hands and feet as well as breathing problems such as asthma.

Diffuse conditions such as muscular aches, fatigue and depression can also arise from **chronic tension**.

You may have consulted your GP about your symptoms and have been advised that you are suffering from anxiety and tension, for which there is no specific cure. He or she may have suggested you try anti-depressant medicine, as there are many new preparations on the market. Are you wondering if this is the right way for you? You may wish to consider all the options before deciding on your approach.

Herbal medicine is the leading alternative to orthodox drug treatments. It is especially favourable to conditions such as anxiety and tension which may have a number of symptoms and respond well to wholistic treatment.

As a member of the National Institute of Medical Herbalists for ten years, I have treated a great number of people with stress related disorders in my clinic. In retail practice I have answered countless queries and given general advice on how to deal with anxiety and tension problems. In this book I have written down the answers to the most frequently asked questions. I offer practical advice on how to treat these conditions, when to consult your doctor and how orthodox as well as herbal medicines work. By reading this book you can:

- Find out how to use herbs to help you relax and relieve symptoms of anxiety.
- Learn how to make simple herbal remedies at home.
- Learn how to understand the labels on remedies you buy in shops.
- Understand the medications your doctor may prescribe for you.

A brief guide to the processes which happen when you are anxious or tense will make you more confident in discussing your health with professionals.

The advice contained in this book is meant to be for general use only. If you have a specific medical condition or an allergy, or are taking medication which may affect your use of herbal medicine, you should consult a qualified health care professional such as a doctor or a medical herbalist before starting to use herbal remedies at home.

Jill Wright

1

Understanding Anxiety and tension

All about the nervous system

There are two parts to the nervous system:

- the **fibres** which carry **nervous impulses**
- and the **chemicals** which are released along these fibres, which extend all over the body, to every internal organ and to the very tips of our fingers and toes.

Nerve fibres in the brain allow us to be aware of what we do – by inter-connecting with specialised centres in the front part of the brain known as the **cortex**. When we reach out to pick up a cup we can do this action slowly or quickly, stop and restart, by thought control. This is called **voluntary action**.

Nerve fibres in the spinal cord allow certain actions to carry on by connecting with the lower parts of the brain, where there are no consciousness centres, so that digestive and breathing movements can take place without our awareness. These are called **involuntary actions**. Walking is also largely an involuntary action – if it weren't we would fall over if we started talking at the same time!

Nerve fibres can be very long, but they generally consist of segments, with small gaps called **synapses** between them. Messenger chemicals are made at these synapses and enable an electrical current to pass along the fibres, which are 'insulated' with a fatty substance called **myelin**. The fibres connect with each other via branch-like extensions of their main cell, which is at the end nearest the brain. Nerve cells in the brain cortex have huge numbers of branches, called **dendrites**, whereas those in the lower brain area have far fewer. These interconnections in the cortex are one of the means by which emotional centres affect the **involuntary digestive muscles** and the general tone of **voluntary muscles**.

Spinal nerves

Nerve fibres end in specialised branches which either receive signals (**receptors**) or pass signals to muscles (**effectors**). There are several types of receptors for heat, cold, pain etc. These activate electrical current, which passes up to the spine or brain and passes down again to an effector, causing a **muscle action**. This is called a **neuronal arc**. Where this doesn't involve brain awareness, it is called an **autonomic action**. Breathing and digestive movements are of this sort. Where an action happens before awareness, it is called a **reflex.** One example of a reflex action is withdrawing your hand from something hot if you touch it by accident.

The cranial nerves

Nerve fibres from the brain are called **cranial nerves**.
Some of these serve one function, such as vision or smell,
others provide a direct link from the thinking part of the
brain to several organs in the body. The **vagus nerve** is the
most important in this respect. It travels from the brain to
the lungs, heart, digestive tract, as well as the liver, spleen
and kidneys. When stress causes anxiety and tension in
emotional centres in the brain, the vagus nerve conveys its
effects to these internal organs. Nervous system chemicals
– **neurotransmittors** – which carry these messages can be
divided into two groups, examples are given below.

Chemical messengers around the body	*Chemical messengers in the brain*
Acetylcholine	GABA
Adrenaline	Serotonin
Glutamic acid	Noradrenaline
	Dopamine

Neurotransmission in the brain

There are a number of chemicals which act as transmitters
in the brain; they are generally known as **neuropeptides**.
They appear to be responsible for the level of activity in
the interconnecting nerve fibres. Only the main ones are
mentioned here as examples. More information is given in
Chapter 2 on conventional medicines.

Neurotransmission around the body

The effects of these chemicals are classified in two groups:
1. **sympathetic** – mainly adrenaline
2. **parasympathetic** – acetylcholine.

The spinal nerves carry sympathetic impulses to internal organs and the vagus nerve carries parasympathetic stimulation to the internal organs.

Sympathetic neurotransmission

Adrenaline and **noradrenaline** are produced in nerve synapses and also in the **adrenal glands**, which sit just on top of the kidneys. It is these which produce 'butterflies' in nervousness and shocks. These chemicals are produced when the brain perceives a threat – physical or verbal attack, or any substitute, such as threatening letters or exams. They enable the famous ' fight or flight' reaction. Adrenaline effects include:

- Blood sugar raised – for instant energy.
- Breathing and heart rate raised – to serve leg and arm muscles.
- Digestive secretions stop, mouth dries.
- Sweating increases, hair stands on end.
- Desire to urinate increases, then less urine is made.
- Desire to defecate increases, then sphincters tighten and movement stops.

Parasympathetic neurotransmission

Acetylcholine is produced in nerve synapses quite near to the organs which the nerve fibres serve. It increases secretions throughout the digestive system, opposes the action of adrenaline, slowing the heart and increasing digestive movements. It causes relaxation of sphincters – muscular rings closing the bowel and bladder – so that they can empty. This is the neurotransmittor of relaxation!

The emotional life of the brain

Emotions are feelings of pain or pleasure, which affect the way we behave. Most of these arise due to stimulation of the specialised areas of the brain, in particular a group of nerve cells called the **hypothalamus**, which is at the heart of a number of nerve cell groups called the **limbic system**. This system has a direct connection to our senses – sight, smell and hearing.

The hypothalamus has a number of functions.

- It acts as a 'search engine' to recall memories.
- Damage to this area causes old memories to be lost.
- It controls hunger and thirst sensations and produces chemicals which determine the rate at which hormones are produced in the pituitary gland of the brain. These affect the water balance, blood pressure, growth rate, sex hormones, thyroid and adrenal hormones.

Nervous impulses from all over the brain as well as the limbic system stimulate the hypothalamus. This helps to explain how emotional responses to stress can affect various systems in the body via stimulation of the hypothalamus.

An overview of the nervous system

- **Brain cortex** – awareness, planning, memory
- **Hypothalamus** – hunger, thirst, sleep, temperature, hormone regulators
- **Limbic system** – emotions, links to sight, smell, hearing
- **Conscious actions** – arms, legs, talking, thinking
- **Autonomic actions** – digestion, breathing
- **Reflex actions** – avoiding pain
- **Sympathetic nerve transmission** – **adrenaline** –action, fight or flight
- **Parasympathetic nerve transmission** – **acetylcholine** – relaxation, secretion, digestion, elimination.
- **Neurotransmission in the brain** – **neuropeptides** – level of activity, interconnections between brain centres.

Anxiety and tension explained

Anxiety is a feeling derived from two basic states of mind; fear and wariness. These are feelings which are common to higher animals and humans. The human emotional system, whilst enormously complex, evolved from the need to respond to basic events – threats from predators, mating, rest, protection of young and hunting for food.

Stress

Threatening predators have been replaced by angry bosses, exams, noisy neighbours, aggressive motorists, redundancy and unemployment to name but a few. Careful watching over young humans hasn't changed much, but has become more complex! Hunting has changed into daily work in exchange for money. Mating is still, for teenagers, a time of uncertainty and competition, with the complications of fashion, education and consumer goods thrown in. Rest and sleep are meant to balance the other activities but city lights and noise may prevent deep sleep for many people. Television and video may bring distressing events into our resting hours and displace relaxing activity.

All these modern versions of threatening predators are called **stress**. Despite our sophistications, our responses to threat and our need to be alert are all created by the same autonomic nervous system which served our pre-hominid ancestors. These reactions are initiated, sometimes to the detriment of our health, by information received in the brain cortex by our senses.

Physical effects of anxiety

Faced with an angry boss, a testing interview or an irate motorist, our mouth dries, skin feels cold, our heart beats faster. We may sweat profusely, muscles receive extra blood (diverted from digestive organs) and tense up as the sympathetic nerves and the adrenal glands respond to this threat. In some people, repeated stress causes overactivity of the parasympathetic nerves, possibly in rebound reaction to excess adrenal levels. This causes acid regurgitation, faster bowel motions, mucus production and even sebum production with acne.

Anticipation of threats such as those described above is what gives rise to anxiety and emotional tension, with permanent tension in muscles. This can give rise to aches and pains, or easily strained muscles, as well as tics and twitches. Pains in the chest muscles caused by emotional tension can be alarming, but don't necessarily herald heart attack.

Behavioural effects of anxiety

Over-anxious people jump at sudden noises and worry about possible disasters in the future. They 'cross bridges' before they meet them and often complain of being unable to concentrate. Many suffer from insomnia, either being unable to get off to sleep, or waking frequently during the night. For some people nightmares disrupt sleep. Some people eat more, most eat less.

A common complaint is worsening symptoms at the weekend, often with headaches.This may be because people are unable to follow their usual routine of response to circulating adrenalin as they are obliged to relax. Sometimes the demands of family life are even more strenuous than work and become an additional, intolerable stress.

Is depression linked to anxiety?

Many doctors link anxiety with **depression** and it is often treated with anti-depressant medicines because they relieve anxious symptoms. Depression causes everything to be slowed, quite literally depressed. Speech, movement and digestion are slowed, even immune-cell production is reduced. This gives the classic run-down condition in which frequent infections such as colds occur.

Exogenous depression

Depression may be linked with the primeval behaviour of frustration, defeat and rejection by the social group. Prolonged stress and anxiety can cause a feeling of hopelessness and lack of motivation. This is called **exogenous** or **reactive depression**, because it is caused by factors outside the body such as stress, shock, bereavement etc.

Endogenous depression

Endogenous depression is thought to be due to an imbalance or deficiency of the body's own hormones. Endogenous depression occurs in many women just before the onset of menstruation, when it is often referred to as part of PMT. It may involve intense feelings of self-loathing and even self-destructive motivation, eating disorders and other features, but fortunately this type of depression is mainly short-lived.

It has been found that helping the brain to preserve such neuropeptides as serotonin and noradrenaline can relieve both anxiety and depression, so it would appear that there is a close link between anxiety and depression. It is also not always clear where to draw the line between exogenous and endogenous depression.

Depressive illnesses which interfere with the ability to run one's own life are outside the scope of this book. The remedies described here are for people suffering from mild depression who are still able to function socially, are able to work, and interact with their families. Using herbal remedies for this type of depression may prevent it worsening into a serious problem.

How anxiety and tension cause other disorders

The problems caused by chronic anxiety and tension can be widespread – you have already read about the effects of adrenaline in fight or flight reactions (page 14). The effects of stress reactions can be seen in various organs and systems.

The skin

Effects of tension show up in the skin as eczema, psoriasis and rashes, even acne. No one really understands how this happens. One theory is that blood vessel constriction in the skin (caused by adrenaline) deprives the skin of essential nutrients. It is also possible that growth and repair are interrupted, or that the adrenal hormones used in this process are diverted to stress reactions. A favourite herbalists' theory is that the elimination of metabolic waste is reduced by some mechanism affecting the lymph and venous supply. Sweating also encourages sebum production, which can increase dandruff and acne.

Female hormone production is also affected by the change in adrenal output, and this can increase acne. It is well known that severe anxiety and shock can inhibit a woman's menstrual cycle. This may happen because the adrenal glands fail to convert precursors – chemical building blocks – into female hormones when they are busy making stress reaction hormones.

Muscles and joints

Muscles are normally held in a state of semi-tension called 'tone', so that they will respond when needed for movement. When we are very anxious, this muscular tension is increased as part of the fight or flight reaction. If not relieved by exercise, this extra tension can cause deep aching, twitches and tics as well as an increased tendency to sprains and strains. These problems may be compounded by reduced elimination of waste products from the muscles into lymph and out from the body.

Digestion

Prolonged anxiety and tension can cause problems in the gut wall similar to those in the skin: low blood perfusion, excessive secretion, poor growth and repair, which may even cause ulceration. High muscular tension causes constipation or diarrhoea, as the muscles fail to act in a gentle, coordinated manner. Small 'rabbit pellet' stools indicate spasmodic muscular movement. Frequent, loose bowel motions are also associated with emotional tension, but may indicate other bowel conditions and need to be investigated by a doctor before treating with home remedies.

Measuring anxiety, tension and depression

If your suffering from depression or anxiety results in you taking time off work you may be referred to an occupational psychiatrist to determine whether you are fit to return. Many doctors, especially those involved in occupational psychiatry, use mood assessment scales, which are based on most of the symptoms mentioned here already. The most well known is called the Hamilton Scale. These scales include questions about one's daily mood, relationships with others, appetite, weight and sexual functions. They can be a useful diagnostic tool but are usually combined with a physical check-up to exclude other causes of symptoms such as thyroid problems.

You may have experienced many of the symptoms described in this chapter and be considering treatment. In the next two chapters we outline what may be available for you.

2

What conventional medicine can offer

There has been an explosion in patient demands and doctors' prescribing for anxiety and depression. This has led to further development in drugs for these disorders. The growing trend is to treat depression rather than anxiety, as the older tranquillisers proved to have unfortunate side effects, in particular dependence. The newest drugs available are the SSRIs. Millions of people take them and new varieties are being researched and marketed regularly. If you visit your doctor with anxiety or depression, you may be offered a variety of medicines including:

- **anxiolytics/ tranquillisers.**
- **hypnotics.**
- **sedatives.**
- **anti-depressants.**

Anxiolytics or tranquillisers

Anxiolytics are also known as tranquillisers. When they are strong enough to induce sleep they are called hypnotics. Sedatives are a type of tranquilliser which would make you unable to perform functions which involved concentration or alertness, such as reading or driving, however you could remain awake and aware of your surroundings. The main types are

- benzodiazepines
- and barbiturates.

Hypnotics

This group includes the benzodiazepines which include nitrazepam, temazepam, flurazepam (brand name Dalmare), flumitrazepam (brand name Rohypnol) and lormetazepam. These are all used as sleeping pills or hypnotics.

Stronger benzodiazepine sedatives are used during the daytime as well. These include diazepam (brand name Valium), aprazolam (brand name Xanax), bromazepam (brand name Lexotan) lorazepam and oxazepam.

How they work

Benzodiazepines increase the action of a neurotransmittor in the brain called **GABA**. This chemical reduces nerve message transmission in the brain, so reduction of its action affects the level of consciousness and slows reactions. This also produces changes in the brain areas responsible for feelings – the **limbic system**. The effect is almost immediate.

Disadvantages

Benzodiazepines remain in the body after a night's sleep, so cause a 'fuzzy' feeling in the morning. The body gets used to their effects and adjusts by producing more excitatory neurotransmittors, so more benzodiazepine is needed to subdue them. This is called **tolerance**, it occurs from three days' to two weeks' use. When you stop taking benzodiazepines, the lack of GABA inhibition causes your brain to be exposed to new, much higher levels of excitatory chemicals, so withdrawal symptoms such as insomnia, tremor, high anxiety, nightmares and even hallucinations can occur.

Sometimes these drugs have the opposite effect to that desired, causing anxiety and aggression. This may be due to inhibition of other chemicals in the brain.

Sedatives

Barbiturates

The main names are amytal, seconal, tuinal and phenobarbitone. These are rarely prescribed now, having been replaced by the newer benzodiazepines. They are sedative to hypnotic in effect, so generally used at night for insomnia and they are still used for epilepsy.

How they work

Barbiturates interfere with the passage of all nerve transmission in the brain, especially increasing GABA, so all functions are affected.

Disadvantages

People become highly dependent on barbiturates very quickly. They are dangerous in overdose because they slow the breathing rate excessively. Barbiturates accumulate in the body, so accidental overdose is easy. Coming off them has to be managed very carefully as severe withdrawal symptoms such as insomnia and delirium occur if they are stopped abruptly. Convulsions and death can occur.

Anti-depressants

There are three main types of anti-depressant:
- **tricyclics.**
- **MAOIs.**
- **SSRIs.**

Tricyclics

Tricyclic anti-depressants are mildly sedative, so are generally taken at night. Their name comes from their chemical structure.

The main names are amitryptiline, amoxapine, clomipramine (brand name Anafranil), dothiepin (brand name Prothiaden), imipramine and trimipramine.

How they work

Tricyclics lift the mood by preventing the destruction of neuro-transmittor chemicals such as noradrenaline, which keep the brain alert. They prevent transmission of acetylcholine at other sites, which gives the mild sedative effect.

Disadvantages
Tricyclics cause dryness in the mouth and blurred vision which can be distressing. This effect wears off in many people, as does the anti-depressant effect.

MAOIs – monoamine oxidase inhibitors

These anti-depressants are particularly useful for relieving anxiety without causing sedation.

How they work
MAOIs help to preserve monoamines in the brain. These are chemicals which increase brain activity, for example alertness, motivation and general sympathetic nervous activity such as constriction of blood vessels (**vasoconstriction**).

Disadvantages
Monoamines also exist in cheese, wine and fermented foods such as soya sauce and Marmite. If these chemical compounds are not destroyed in the normal way, by monoamine oxidase, they can cause severe vasoconstriction and dangerously high blood pressure. These drugs are not normally used nowadays since they have been replaced by SSRIs.

SSRIs – selective serotonin re-uptake inhibitors

These are the newest drugs available to treat anxiety and depression. They are very widely prescribed to all age-groups. The main names are fluoxetine (brand name Prozac), paroxetine (brand name Seroxat), setraline (brand name Lustral).

How they work

SSRIs prevent the destruction of **serotonin**, which is a chemical involved in patterns of sleep as well as alertness and confident, energetic feelings, the sort of feelings associated with waking from hibernation!

Disadvantages

Insomnia is a common problem with SSRIs. Nausea, loss of appetite and severe headaches are common in the first few weeks of use but these symptoms usually subside. One of the most under-reported side effects is a mildly euphoric feeling which sets in after two to three months' use, which allows users to behave a little more boldly than they ought. Making over-confident decisions and being licentious in speech is common. This behaviour occurs because of the complete suppression of anxiety, which is, in small doses, an essential component of social judgement.

Other therapies

In addition to prescribing medicines, many doctors' surgeries now employ counsellors and psychotherapists, to whom they refer patients for talking therapies. Many patients refer themselves to psychotherapists or counsellors. These types of therapy are referred to briefly in this book but it is beyond the scope of this book to go into any of them in detail.

3

Using herbs to treat anxiety and tension

Herbal medicine is the leading alternative to orthodox medicine, for treating anxiety, tension and depression. It is used all over the world for emotional problems and has a very ancient history in treatments for this type of condition.

When modern herbalists write a prescription for an anxious or tense patient they try to treat the body and mind together, relieving **systemic** as well as **emotional** symptoms.

Aims of herbal treatment

- reduce emotional tension
- relieve muscular tension
- lower blood pressure
- relax and improve digestion
- relieve skin irritation
- improve immunity
- improve sleep
- reduce fatigue
- relieve pains.

This sounds complicated but, by careful choosing, you can make up a compound remedy which suits you. You may need to experiment a little but none of the herbs mentioned in this book are dangerous. Sample remedies are presented later with the case histories (Chapter 7), and there is a list of Sources and Resources on page 121.

How herbs work

Herbs contain small quantities of chemicals, compared to modern pharmaceutical products which extract or synthesise one chemical in much larger amounts. This means there is no danger of sudden physiological changes which cause side-effects. Valerian, for example appears to improve the quality of your sleep as well as helping you to doze off and doesn't cause a sluggish feeling in the morning unlike many pharmaceutical products. This is because the chemicals it contains are in very small amounts and don't last long in the body. This lower level of activity may be disappointing if you want to be 'knocked out ' but using herbs like valerian as part of a plan to restore sleep patterns can be an effective alternative to stronger single chemicals like the well-known sedative, valium (derived originally from valerian).

Most herbs contain a large number of active constituents which work together to create one or more effects.The more we find out about herbs, the more we realise that each constituent is a valued part of the whole, negative effects balanced by positive ones. A good example follows.

Recently much has been made of a research trial which showed that a St John's wort preparation made liver enzymes more active, which reduced the effect of other drugs taken at the same time because they were metabolised before reaching their target. The St John's wort preparation used was standardised to contain a larger amount of one constituent – hypericin – than all the others. Not only has hypericin failed to show anti-depressant activity on its own in repeated trials, but another ingredient – hyperforin – has been shown to counterbalance hypericin in its effect on liver enzymes. Many other research trials on St John's wort have shown no adverse effect on other drugs and doctors in Germany continue to prescribe it as a favoured anti-depressant.

Similar bad publicity surrounds liquorice, where glycyrrhizin is thought to raise blood pressure, but in fact dozens of other constituents act to lower it, in particular by diuresis (elimination of water).

There are many more examples of this sort of balanced action. Where two or more constituents act together to create the same effect this is known as synergy. These are particular features of herbal medicine which enable it to support the wholistic approach very well.

How long herbs take to work?

Although some herbs act swiftly, like the relaxant valerian, herbal remedies generally act slowly and their effect is cumulative. They gently rebalance physiological processes, as though switch after switch is thrown until the full effect is achieved. This can take weeks, sometimes months, but it is worth waiting for, as the risk of side-effects is very low due to the tiny amounts of chemicals involved.

How do herbal remedies get to their target ?

Herbal compounds need to be absorbed across the wall of the digestive tract, so they have to be released from their structures (stem, root, leaf, flower or berry etc) first of all. Hot water and alcohol do some of this job for us, so that teas and tinctures are more easily absorbed than tablets and capsules, which need to be broken down physically before the active chemicals are separated from the inert matter to which they are attached. All food and medicine passes through the liver (in the blood circulation) before it finally enters the body tissues, where it is used.

Sometimes chemical compounds need help in crossing through the wall of the digestive tract into the blood stream. Carrier chemicals can be attached to compounds and ferry them through channels in the gut lining. Hydrochloride is frequently found to be part of conventional drug names as it has this function.

Herbal compounds often have an advantage over synthesised chemicals in this respect, as they have naturally occurring carrier chemicals already attached to them. This is what is meant by affinity. Herbs are said to have a greater affinity for the human body, like spare parts dedicated to a particular engine made by the same manufacturer.

Are herbs safe?

All the herbs which British Herbalists use are safe when used in the correct dose for the right ailment. The herbs mentioned in this book have been selected for their safety in untrained hands, although you may need professional help with your diagnosis. The National Institute of Medical Herbalists (NIMH – see page 123) maintains an extensive data bank and works with government watchbodies to ensure safety of its herbs. Recently some attention was given to the group of compounds called pyrrolizidine alkaloids, present in several plants including comfrey, because they can cause (reversible) damage to the liver if ingested in large quantities. The evidence on comfrey is not based on human case studies and the research involved feeding rats exclusively on large amounts of comfrey. There is only one reported case of human toxicity world-wide, which concerned a woman who took comfrey tea many times a day concurrently with illegal drugs in high doses over a long period. Several governments, including that of Britain, made moves to ban its use. After extensive discussions with the NIMH, it was agreed to limit use to the guidelines given above, and restrict the root (which contains more PAs) to external use only. In this way herbalists acknowledge the potential risk and demonstrate the history of safe use.

Combining herbs with orthodox medication

Some drugs are altered by liver enzymes, so that they enter the main blood circulation in a different form. Some herbs (especially **bitters**) stimulate the liver cells to work harder, or cause more liver cells to be active and this can affect other drugs because the liver removes them from circulation before they have had a chance to do their work. Digoxin is one of these and is also a drug with a 'narrow therapeutic window'. This means that the difference between an insufficient, a beneficial and a harmful dose is very small, so that small changes in the amount getting through to the bloodstream may result in the drug not working as it should. Two other drugs like this are Cyclosporin, used to prevent transplant rejection, and Phenytoin, an anti-epileptic. It is very important to check with a qualified herbalist and let your doctor know if you are adding herbal medicine to medication you are currently using.

There are many herbs which can be taken safely with other medicines, so don't feel deterred from trying, but do seek professional advice. Herbs can be used to offset the side-effects of necessary medication, like indigestion or nausea. They may enable you to take less of a remedy which you need, but which has troublesome side-effects. The important thing is how you feel, and that you don't endanger your health. It may be simple to ask your doctor to monitor blood levels of drugs and adjust the dose if necessary.

It would not be wise to embark on herbal medicine without medical supervision if you are on anti-psychotic medication, as you may not be aware that your mental condition has deteriorated when your current medication ceases to work. You may have strong feelings about the disadvantages of your drugs, but may not realise how your behaviour is changing and affecting others badly. It is possible to have herbal medicine for other complaints while on medication for psychosis, but you must consult your doctor first and allow yourself to be monitored.

If you are on chemotherapy for cancer, it would be better to wait until your treatment has finished before taking herbal medicine, unless you are looking for help with troublesome side effects such as nausea or diarrhoea. Several herbs can help here without reducing the effectiveness of your anti-cancer drugs.

Drugs to be careful with	*Conditions to be careful with*
Digoxin	Pregnancy
Phenytoin	Epilepsy
Anti-psychotics	Schizophrenia, psychosis
Immune suppressants	Organ transplants
Anti-cancer drugs	Allergies

Sometimes over the counter herbal medicines are labelled with contra-indications. This is required by law in Germany. It means for example that you will be told if you shouldn't take the medicine if you are pregnant, taking another specific medication, have an allergy or a certain medical condition. This will become more common throughout Europe in the near future.

The advantages of using whole plant preparations

Herbalists insist on using whole, unaltered products to guarantee the sort of benefits we claim for them. We believe that plants would only have gained a historical reputation for certain effects if their constituents were robust enough to maintain the same effect wherever they were grown or whatever minor differences there might be between local plant populations. If only one variety in one particular year made someone feel better, its reputation would not have stood the test of time.

The current trend, based on scientific research, is to standardise the process of growing, harvesting and storing herbs, so that their use is sustainable and patients get the best value from them. Medical herbalists also recommend using whole, unaltered preparations, as nature presented them, so that each constituent is represented in its natural amounts. This is the type of preparation on which traditional knowledge is based. It is also useful to remember that patients vary much more than plants do!

The affinity of herbs

Many herbs show a greater affinity for the human body than synthetic medicines. This is because they have compounds and molecules attached which make them more easily absorbed into body cells and tissues. These are often in the sugar family. Some are known as glycosides and these and their relatives, monosaccharides, are attracting a lot of interest in the modern research world. These carrier chemicals enable herbal compounds to enter target cells more easily, and may explain how herbs can have an effect, even at quite low doses.

The constituents of herbs

Another advantage of herbal medicine is that there are so many different plants with similar actions, but different combinations of constituents. You can change from one to the other to avoid becoming tolerant or developing sensitivities. For example, there are many relaxing herbs, each with its own supplementary actions, including hormonal, diuretic, anti-spasmodic and anti-inflammatory effects.

Limeflowers lowers blood pressure by dilating blood vessels; lemon balm relaxes the muscles of the gut as well as reducing wind: chamomile eases acid indigestion: St John's wort is anti-inflammatory, cramp bark relieves muscle cramps.

These actions of herbs are called their **applications**. Just as ideas about emotional problems have changed, so names for herbal medicines used in treating them have altered. In most herbals you will find a variety of terms such as nervines, nervous restoratives, anxiolytics, relaxants, adaptogens, thymoleptics, tonics and tropho-restoratives for all the major organs including the nervous system. Nowadays herbalists also refer to the anti-depressant actions of herbs, although this seems to replace several older terms which are still used.

Herbal applications

Herbal remedies include un-conventional applications such as:

- nervous restoratives
- relaxants
- hypnotics
- anxiolytics
- adaptogens
- immuno-stimulants
- tonics
- diuretics
- anti-spasmodics
- vasodilators.

These are herbs whose actions are not found in conventional drug descriptions. Mostly this is because of their complexity, which is best reflected in the older names for their applications.

Nervous restoratives

These are also referred to as nervine tropho-restoratives, nervine tonics and thymoleptics. This is the group whose actions have been renamed anti-depressant. They are thought to improve the functioning of the nervous system and lift the mood (thymos = mood in ancient Greek). Some of these may help restore the tissues, for example repairing the damage done by diabetes or to the peripheral nerves. Their effects might be to relieve twitches or temporary paralysis. Skullcap, oats St John's wort and betony have some traditional reputation for this.

Relaxants

Relaxant herbs relieve the feeling of anxiety by inhibiting certain brain chemicals which perpetuate the anxious state of mind. They induce relaxation without a sedating effect, and give a feeling of well-being but don't affect social judgement.

Herbal relaxants relieve tension and restore nervous activity to a normal level, whereas sedatives reduce brain activity to below normal functioning level. Relaxation can improve concentration rather than impairing it, so it is a good example of a balancing action for which herbs are well known. These herbs work in two ways:

- Nervine relaxants act centrally, by reducing the brain's sensitivity to nerve messages from the periphery (skin, joints, muscles etc).
- Muscle relaxants act peripherally (on nerve centres in the spinal cord, or on nerve endings in the skin), reducing the number of messages sent from the periphery to the brain.

Many herbal relaxants act both centrally and peripherally.

Hypnotics

Hypnotics are sedatives which are strong enough to send you to sleep. Valerian is the most famous, but it is not as strong as orthodox hypnotics. Most herbs do not gain in hypnotic effect if you increase the dose much above the standard.

Anxiolytics

This is an old term for relaxant herbs. As the name suggests, they are supposed to reduce feelings of anxiety.

Adaptogens

Adaptogenic herbs improve the body's functions, helping it to cope with stress. This often involves stimulating the adrenal glands or mimicking their action. Adaptogens also improve immunity and feelings of energy, possibly by better utilisation of nutrients and increasing metabolism. General adaptogenic herbs such as ginseng are not well understood. It is possible that some of their constituents, such as saponins, open cells to allow hormones and stress-response chemicals in and out. This is also the action which helps to reduce fatigue.

Immuno-stimulants

Some herbs increase the effectiveness of the immune system, by stimulating the production of immune cells or making them more effective. There is new research to show that herbs such as echinacea do this by enabling immune cells to attach to invading organisms – viruses and bacteria – better. Aromatic herbs appear to have a unique anti-viral effect, giving protection against infections such as influenza, warts and herpes. It is thought that they remain in body tissues, making their cells in some way inaccessible to infective agents and that they penetrate the coating of viral agents. This effect doesn't last long, so these herbs have to be taken every day for a period of time to avoid infection. Many asthmatics benefit from taking a variety of aromatic herbal teas regularly to avoid infections which trigger severe asthma.

Tonics

Tonic herbs improve the function of specific organs, usually by increasing their activity. For example, liver tonics increase enzyme action and bile production. Digestive tonics increase digestive secretion and improve muscle movements. Kidney tonics increase the elimination of urine. Nerve tonics enable better functioning of the nervous system with very mild stimulant effects.

Diuretics

Diuretics increase elimination of water via the kidneys.

Anti-spasmodics

Anti-spasmodics relieve tension in muscles of limbs and internal organs.

Vasodilators

Vasodilators allow blood vessels to expand, which generally reduces blood pressure.

The alternative approach

You will need to use a number of strategies, as well as herbal medicine, to achieve long-term control over the effects of stress.

Relaxation therapies

You may be aware of the rapid growth in relaxation therapies available. If you visit your local alternative complementary therapy clinic you will probably find an impressive list. They can be grouped into **physical** and **talking therapies**.

Physical therapies – body work

These are aimed at relieving the physical effects of stress, by reducing muscle tension, increasing blood flow and clearing metabolic waste products (toxins). This group includes:

- reflexology
- acupuncture
- massage/aromatherapy.

Relaxation exercises are a very popular and extremely good way of combating stress, anxiety and tension. Yoga is excellent for this and you will be able to find classes in your local area. This is a very ancient system of exercise which involves breathing and muscle stretching routines as well as meditation. Some complementary therapy clinics offer courses specifically in relaxation techniques which are mainly derived from yoga. Some churches include relaxation classes in their social outreach programmes.

The important thing about relaxation exercises is to learn a routine which you can do every day at home or at work, so that relaxing becomes a habit.

Regular use of bodywork therapies is extremely useful in establishing and maintaining an improvement in physical condition. The body is re-trained to acquire the habit of relaxing by repetition. On-going sessions help body and mind to adjust to a more balanced condition by easing muscular tension, helping to eliminate toxins, and improving breathing and circulation.

Talking therapies – mind work
These are aimed at changing the way you think and behave, so that stress doesn't cause physical or mental problems. The objective may be to improve confidence and assertiveness or recognise weaknesses and triggers. This group includes;

- counselling
- psychotherapy
- spiritual healing
- hypnosis.

Mindwork approaches should be able to offer a course of sessions with a finite end as this is basically a learning process about yourself. You should be able to take notes and review your progress as with any other learning experience. Make sure you understand the aims and outcomes of this sort of treatment and ask how your practitioner records your progress. Check that you understand how you will recognise change.

Most complementary therapy clinics have open days, phone up and ask when your local clinic has theirs. On an open day you ought to be able to sample some of the bodywork therapies or listen to short lectures on each subject. Individual practitioners should have brochures which explain their therapies thoroughly and set out the expected timescale for treatment. There are lots of books on complementary therapies available from local libraries and bookshops.

Most local education authorities offer evening classes and part-time courses in reflexology, aromatherapy and massage. This is a very rewarding and economical way of including bodywork therapies in your life on a regular basis. You can meet regularly to swap treatments with your friends, or offer simple relaxing treatments to your family. In this way you will have acquired a long-lasting tool for dealing with stress in your life and a way of helping others.

🍃 4 🍃

Directory of useful herbs

You will need to use a number of strategies to relieve anxiety and tension. Preventive approaches are covered in Chaper 6 on eating to counteract the effect of stress. You can use the information in this section to select the right herbs. The case histories in Chapter 7 guide you in building classic remedies or tailoring one to your own individual needs.

Herbs are usually categorised by their actions, and each herb will have some primary and some secondary actions. In some the actions are of equal importance. To treat anxiety and tension you may need nervous restoratives, relaxants, hypnotics, adaptogens, immuno-stimulants and tonics. When you read the case histories later you will see how this directory can be used to pick herbs from the various categories.

NERVOUS RESTORATIVES

Betony	Oats	Skullcap
St John's wort		

Betony

Latin name   Stachys betonica

Origin	Europe
Part used	Leaf and flower
Dose	1 teaspoon per cup, 1-3 times daily
	Tincture 4ml, 1-3 times daily
Constituents	Alkaloids, choline, tannins
Primary actions	Nervine relaxant
	Pain reliever
Secondary actions	Bitter tonic
	Wound healer
How it works	The alkaloids (similar to those in oats) are responsible for the mildly sedative and pain relieving effects. They are also bitter. This causes an increase in digestive secretions, especially from the liver. The tannins may be the source of its wound healing effects, which were noted to heal internal wounds such as stomach ulcers.
Growing guide	Betony prefers the damp, dappled shade of woodland.

Oats

Latin name	Avena sativa
Origin	Europe and worldwide
Part used	Seeds (grains)
Dose	2-3 tablespoons daily
	Tincture 5ml, 3 times daily
Constituents	Alkaloids, starch, flavonoids, coumarins, minerals including calcium, iron, zinc, vitamins B, E, saponins, glycosides
Primary action	Nervous restorative
	Adaptogen

Secondary action   Topical emollient

How it works   Oats has a long tradition of use in debilitated conditions, where the person is 'worn to a frazzle'. The alkaloids are mildly stimulant to muscles, but the herb is frequently added to calming mixtures. Its coumarins reduce muscle spasm in the digestive tract. Starch provides long-lasting energy and soothes the surfaces it touches (digestive tract and skin). Minerals and vitamins contribute to the restoration of health. Saponins open cells and allow greater interchange of messenger chemicals. Glycosides also help to transport medicinal compounds into body cells where they are needed. Oat starch is noted for its effect in reducing cholesterol deposits in the blood stream. Oats has also acquired a reputation for helping to relieve nicotine withdrawal symptoms.

Growing guide   Large field needed, only for the enthusiast! Oats will tolerate the poor soil and lower temperatures of northern hillsides.

Skullcap

Latin name   Scutellaria laterifolia

Origin   America

Part used   Leaf

Dose   1 teaspoon per cup, 1-2 cups per day
Tincture 3ml, 1-3 times daily

Constituents   Flavonoids, glycosides, iridoids, volatile oil,

	tannin
Primary action	Relaxant
Secondary actions	Anti-spasmodic
	Anti-inflammatory (possibly)
How it works	Little is known about the active constituents of American skullcap as most research is based on a Chinese variant. We rely on the tradition of use for our knowledge of its actions. The anti-inflammatory effect is present in the Chinese variety and it is very likely that both varieties have the same constituents. American skullcap is noted for its central (brain) calming effect. Flavonoids stabilise blood vessel walls and contribute to its mooted anti-inflammatory effect, as well as mildly increasing the elimination of water via the kidneys. It has a long traditional use for neurological diseases such as epilepsy and motor neurone diseases.
Growing guide	Prefers damp soil. Sow under glass and plant out in early summer in a warm, damp spot (pond-side, bog-garden).

St John's wort

Latin name	Hypericum perforatum
Origin	Europe
Part used	Leaf and flower
Dose	1 teaspoon per cup, 1-2 cups per day
	Tincture 5ml per day
Constituents	Essential oil, hypericin, hyperforin,

	flavonoids, tannins
Primary actions	Nervous restorative
	Relieves anxiety
Secondary action	Anti-inflammatory
How it works	The whole herb produces a calming and uplifting effect, which reduces the perception of pain as well as inhibiting painful processes such as spasm and inflammation. None of the individual constituents have proved to be effective on their own. The oil, applied topically, is anti-inflammatory and analgesic, useful for neuralgia, shingles and earache.
Caution	A recent research trial suggests that St John's wort may make the liver destroy some drugs, which could be important for medicines whose dose has to be very precise, such as anti-epileptics, immune suppressants and heart rhythm regulators. Unfortunately, this research was based on a standardised type of St John's wort, where extra hypericin had been added. No trials using non-modified St John's wort have shown such results, but we now advise patients who are taking any of the medicines above to avoid this herb and grapefruit, which has the same effect to a greater degree. St John's wort is perfectly safe to use externally with any medication except drugs designed to make your skin more sensitive to the sun (some psoriasis sufferers take these).

Growing guide   Easy to sow direct in spring, will tolerate most soils.

RELAXANTS

Black horehound	Kava-kava	Verbena
Catnip	Lemon balm	Vervein
Chamomile	Limeflowers	
Hops	Passionflower	

Black Horehound

Latin name	Ballota nigra
Origin	Europe
Part used	Leaf
Dose	1 teaspoon per cup, 1-3 cups daily
	Tincture 4ml, 1-3 times daily
Constituents	Alkaloids, bitters, volatile oil
Primary action	Sedative
Secondary action	Relieves nausea
How it works	There is little information on how black horehound works. It is often used in morning sickness of pregnancy and nausea associated with ear disorders such as Menières disease or of general nervous origin. It is likely that the action is a result of both alkaloids and volatile oil acting on nerve centres in the brain. It has a very long history of use in Britain and Europe.
Growing guide	Small downy perennial, grows in hedgerows and meadows. It has a strong, rather

unpleasant smell when fresh, this disappears on drying.

Catnip

Latin name	Nepeta cataria
Origin	Europe
Part used	Leaf
Dose	1 teaspoon per cup, 1-3 times daily
	Tincture 4ml 1-3 times daily
Constituents	Volatile oil (including thymol, carvacrol), bitters, tannins
Primary actions	Relaxant
	Relieves fever
Secondary actions	Secongestant
	Anti-spasmodic
How it works	The volatile oil has a decongestant action as well as being sedative. It has an anti-bacterial and anti-spasmodic action in the digestive tract and in the bronchi, because the volatile oil compounds such as thymol diffuse into all body tissues, including the lungs. This is an underrated herb. It is very useful for anxiety and tension in children, especially those with bronchitis or asthma.

Chamomile

Latin name	Matricaria recutita
Origin	Europe
Part used	Flower (This plant has been renamed several times recently, so you must specify small,

	cone-headed flowers with a single row of petals. This is currently called German chamomile)
Dose	1 teaspoon per cup, 1-3 cups per day Tincture 5ml, 1-3 times daily
Primary action	Relaxant
Secondary action	Digestive tonic
Constituents	Volatile oil, flavonoids, coumarins, valerianic acid, sesquiterpene bitters, salicylates, tannins
How it works	Chamomile is one of the most complex herbs in common use. It has a little of almost every action shown by plants. The volatile oil acts on the brain to reduce sensitivity as well as being mildly antiseptic and anti-inflammatory when applied topically. Flavonoids are mildly diuretic, coumarins relax visceral muscle by acting on local nerve centres. The volatile oil is carminative (reduces bacterial ferment and wind in the gut). Sesquiterpene bitters stimulate bile production in the liver and there are bitter glycosides which add to this action. Anti-inflammatory salicylates are present in small quantities, tannins astringe and tone the wall of the gut, alleviating diarrhoea.
Growing guide	Annual. Sow seeds each year in pots or window boxes, or scatter freely in a sunny position in spring.

Hops

Latin name	Humulus lupulus
Origin	Europe
Part used	Strobiles (flower-like parts)
Dose	1 teaspoon per cup, 1-2 cups daily
	Tincture 4ml, 1-3 times daily
Constituents	Bitters, volatile oil, valerianic acid, flavonoids, tannins, oestrogens
Primary actions	Bitter digestive tonic
	Sedative
Secondary actions	Diuretic
	Hormonal agent
How it works	Bitters stimulate digestive secretions, which aids absorption and helps to obtain energy from food. Although fresh hops are much stronger than dried, the sedative effect of the volatile oil does appear to be preserved in the tincture. It is mainly used for insomnia and nervous indigestion. Very useful for debility and fatigue due to lack of sleep.
Growing guide	Very attractive light green rampant climber. Grows from rooted cuttings or layering. Will cover an old tree or fence, but loses its leaves in the winter.

Kava-kava

Latin name	Piper methysticum
Origin	South Sea islands
Part used	Root
Dose	1 teaspoon per cup, 1-2 cups per day

	Tincture 3ml, 1-2 times daily
Constituents	Pyrones, piperidine alkaloids, glycosides, mucilage
Primary actions	Relaxant
	Anti-depressant
Secondary actions	Anti-spasmodic
	Diuretic
How it works	Not much is known about the actions of kava-kava, though research is increasing as it becomes popular. The pyrones and piperidines act centrally (on the brain) to reduce sensitivity to pain. Applied topically it is rubefacient and numbing. It also has a reputation for relieving fatigue, so in some books it is referred to as a stimulant. It is best to view it like alcohol, relaxing and stimulating at the same time, with some effects of intoxication at high doses.
Growing guide	It is not possible to cultivate in the British Isles.

Lemon Balm

Latin name	Melissa officinalis
Origin	Europe
Part used	Leaf
Dose	1 teaspoon per cup, 1-3 cups daily
	Tincture 4ml, 1-3 times daily
Constituents	Volatile oil, flavonoids, phenols, triterpenes, tannins
Primary actions	Relaxant

	Digestive tonic
Secondary actions	Anti-viral
	Anti-thyroid
How it works	The volatile oil has a central relaxing effect (on the brain) as well as reducing thyroid hormone stimulation of other systems. It also inhibits the growth of viruses such as herpes by giving a sort of repellant protection to the tissues, and possibly penetrating viral coating. The phenols add to this effect and help to dispel bacteria in the gut. Triterpenes are bitter, so stimulate digestive secretions. Tannins astringe the wall of the gut, alleviating diarrhoea.
Growing guide	You will rarely have to resort to seed, nearly everyone has some lemon balm to give away. It seeds itself like mad, tolerates any soil and will grow in pots.

Limeflowers

Latin name	Tilia europaea
Origin	Europe
Part used	Leaf and flower
Dose	1 teaspoon per cup, 1-2 cups per day
	Tincture 4ml ,1-3 times daily
Constituents	Volatile oil, flavonoids, phenols, mucilage, tannins
Primary actions	Relaxant
	Vasodilator
Secondary actions	Diaphoretic (increases sweating)

	Anti-spasmodic
How it works	The volatile oil reduces the brain's sensitivity to pain messages, mucilage soothes the stomach and gut wall and flavonoids make blood vessels less fragile. Phenols are antiseptic and diaphoretic (increase sweating), which induces dilation of blood vessels. The overall effect is to calm and lower blood pressure. Limeflowers is a particularly nice tasting tea.
Growing guide	Too large a tree for the average garden. A most magnificent specimen can be seen at Kew Gardens in London.

Passionflower

Latin name	Passiflora incarnata
Origin	America
Part used	Leaf
Dose	1 teaspoon per cup, 1-2 cups daily
	Tincture 2ml, 1-2 times daily
Constituents	Alkaloids, saponins, flavonoids
Primary actions	Relaxant
	Anti-spasmodic
Secondary action	Vasodilator
How it works	Alkaloids act on the brain, reducing sensitivity to pain. Those in passionflower are known to work on nerves in the spinal cord which control the movement of blood vessel and digestive muscle. This produces a relaxing effect which lowers blood pressure.

The flavonoids supplement vitamin C in strengthening blood vessels by being laid down in the structure of the muscle wall. This also tends to reduce inflammatory swelling as it reduces leakage through capillary walls, and increases elasticity.

Growing guide   Easily grown on a south-facing wall or fence. Trim lightly each spring

Verbena

Latin name	Lippia citriodora
Origin	South America
Part used	Leaf
Dose	1 teaspoon per cup, 1-3 times daily
	Tincture 4ml, 1-3 times daily
Constituents	Essential oils, bitters
Primary action	Relaxant
Secondary action	Relieves fever
How it works	The essential oil is responsible for verbena's calming action and gives the very pleasant, long-lasting lemon scent to this tea. Very mildly bitter compounds reduce temperature and stimulate digestion. This makes an excellent tea for daily use.
Growing guide	Fifteen foot shrub, grows in sheltered positions in Britain (the Isle of Wight has some specimens).

Vervein

Latin name	Verbena officinalis
Origin	Europe
Part used	Leaf, flower
Dose	1 teaspoon per cup, 1-3 cups daily
	Tincture 3ml, 1-3 times daily
Constituents	Glycosides, iridoids, bitters, volatile oil, alkaloids, mucilage
Primary actions	Relaxant
	Bitter digestive tonic
Secondary actions	Anti-depressant
	Anti-viral
How it works	Not all actions are clearly understood. Bitters stimulate liver and digestive secretions, unknown constituents act on the brain to reduce sensitivity to pain and increase feelings of well-being. These are probably found in the volatile oil, which is responsible for the anti-viral effect, acting as a repellant in the tissues of the body. This is known as the 'constitutional effect' which French aromatherapists call the 'terrain theory'. The whole herb has some pain relieving action when applied as a poultice to inflamed joints and muscles.
Growing guide	Sow under glass, plant out in late spring. Vervein is a very delicate looking plant which will seed itself readily in sunny spots.

HYPNOTICS

Poppy	Valerian	Wild lettuce

Poppy

Latin name	Papaver rhoeas
Origin	Europe
Part used	Flower
Dose	1 teaspoon per cup, 1-2 cups daily. Syrup is usually preferred, though hardly obtainable now. You can get tincture of Californian poppy, (Latin name *escholtzia*) which is closely related. To make your own red poppy tincture you need to use the petals straight after picking.
Constituents	Alkaloids, meconic acid, mucilage
Primary actions	Pain reliever
	Anti-spasmodic
Secondary action	Expectorant
How it works	The alkaloids act on the brain to reduce sensitivity to pain messages. Mucilage soothes the gullet and stomach. By reflex action it soothes the bronchial tubes, which assists expectoration.
Growing guide	Sow seed direct in the ground in a sunny, well-drained spot in early spring. Collect and process immediately on flowering.

Valerian

Latin name	Valeriana officinalis

Origin	Europe
Part used	Root
Dose	1 teaspoon per cup, one cup per night
	Tincture 2-5ml nightly
Constituents	Valerianic acid, alkaloids, glycosides, tannins, choline, flavonoids, valepotriates, iridoids
Primary action	Relaxant/sedative
Secondary action	Anti-spasmodic
How it works	Valerianic acid and valepotriates reduce exciteability of the brain and feelings of anxiety. Best used at night as it is on the borderline between relaxants and sedatives. Flavonoids are mildly diuretic (increase water elimination).
Growing guide	Sow directly in a sunny spot with damp soil in early spring.

Wild Lettuce

Latin name	Lactuca virosa
Origin	Europe
Part used	Leaf
Dose	1 teaspoon per cup, 1 cup at night
	Tincture 3ml, 1-2 times daily
Constituents	Alkaloids, bitters, flavonoids, coumarins
Primary actions	Relaxant
	Pain reliever
Secondary actions	Cough relieving
	Anti-spasmodic
How it works	The alkaloids act on the brain, reducing sensitivity to pain messages. Coumarins are

anti-spasmodic, so all muscles relax, (bronchial, digestive, and somatic) tension and irritability are diminished.

Growing guide   Sow seed direct in the ground and allow to flower.

ADAPTOGENS

Borage	Ginseng	Gotu kola

Borage

Latin name	Borago officinalis
Origin	Europe and Africa
Part used	Leaves
Dose	1 teaspoon per cup
	Tincture 4ml, 1-3 times daily
Constituents	Pyrrolizidine alkaloids, choline, mucilage
Primary action	Adaptogen
Secondary action	Diuretic
How it works	It isn't known how borage exerts its action on the adrenal gland but it appears to help conditions where natural cortisone is low, such as vitiligo and past steroid treatment. The pyrrolizidine alkaloids – PAs are present in very small amounts so it has never needed the safety warnings which are attached to comfrey. Borage has a very long reputation for producing a more confident mood.
Caution	Despite the apparent safety of borage, those

who have experienced severe liver disease, such as hepatitis, should avoid using this herb as they may be particularly susceptible to the accumulation of PAs in liver cells.

Growing guide Very easy to grow, sow seed direct into the soil in spring. Self-seeds everywhere, so you will never be without it again.

Ginseng

Latin name Panax ginseng. Also known as Chinese and Korean ginseng

Origin China

Part used Root

Dose $^1/_2$ teaspoon per cup
Tincture 2ml, 1-3 times daily

Constituents Saponin glycosides (ginsenosides), glycans (panaxans), volatile oil

Primary actions Adaptogen
Stimulant

Secondary actions Nervous restorative
Relaxant

How it works The constituents and actions of ginseng are very complex. New facts are emerging regularly from the large amount of research which is carried out into this plant. The ginsenosides increase natural cortisone and stimulate the adrenal gland as well as the hypothalamus. The glycans reduce blood sugar by increasing its uptake and use in cells. Ginseng is considered a little too

	stimulant for long-term use, especially by women.
Caution	People who have high blood pressure should avoid using ginseng as it may aggravate their condition.
Growing guide	There is no record of it being grown successfully in Britain. It is cultivated in China, Korea, America and Japan.

Gotu Kola

Latin name	Centella asiatica
Origin	India
Part used	Leaf
Dose	1/2 teaspoon per cup
	Tincture 2ml, 1-3 times daily
Constituents	Flavonoids, triterpene glycosides, bitters, tannins, alkaloids, volatile oil
Primary actions	Adaptogen
	Nervous restorative
Secondary actions	Sedative
	Skin cleanser
How it works	Although an Asian plant, gotu kola has been used in British herbal medicine for at least 200 years. Research has generally been carried out on whole plant preparations, so its constituents are not fully understood. It is mildly sedative, which may be due to its alkaloids. The saponins are probably responsible for the adrenal tonic action. Its bitters act as a digestive tonic. It has some

very interesting anti-infective actions, notably on leprosy and skin disorders including ulcers and hypertrophic scars (sometimes called keloid). It has been shown to reduce fibrosis and internal adhesions after surgery.

Growing guide   No record of being grown in Britain.

IMMUNO-STIMULANTS

Echinacea	Siberian ginseng

Echinacea

Latin name	Echinacea purpurea
Origin	North America
Part used	Root
Dose	1 teaspoon per cup
	Tincture 4ml, 1-3 times daily
Constituents	Inulin, resin, volatile oil, sterols, polysaccharides, glycosides, alkaloids
Primary actions	Immune stimulant
	Antiseptic
Secondary actions	Digestive stimulant
	Diuretic
How it works	It is now thought that the polysaccharides are responsible for increasing the number and effectiveness of white blood cells (immune cells). Glycosides help to carry chemicals into cells, the alkaloids have an expectorant effect (clearing the lungs) and the volatile oil is very slightly sedative as well as bitter. This

	helps to stimulate digestive secretions and liver functions. Resins are locally antiseptic (as a gargle and on the skin). Inulin is diuretic (increases elimination of water).
Growing guide	This is worth growing for its beautiful pink daisy flower. Easy to grow from seed, but very prone to slug attack, so needs protection.

Siberian Ginseng

Latin name	Eleutherococcus senticosus
Origin	Russia
Part used	Root
Dose	$1/2$ teaspoon per cup
	Tincture 2ml, 1- 2 times daily
Constituents	Saponins – eleutherosides
Primary action	Immunostimulant
Secondary action	Adaptogen
How it works	Siberian ginseng is in the same family as Chinese ginseng but is chemically different. It was given its western name during the 1950s in Russia, when there was intense competition with Chinese and American rivals. Much research was done, showing its ability to reduce sick absence in Russian factories, which may not be entirely reliable. New research has noted that it improves heart performance and dilates blood vessels. It is in wide use in British herbal medicine as an aid to fighting infections and recovery from illness, but the actions are not fully

	understood.
Growing guide	No record of being grown successfully in Britain.

TONICS

Agrimony	Damiana	Poplar
Betony	Dandelion	Rosemary

Agrimony

Latin name	Agrimonia eupatoria
Origin	Europe
Part used	Leaf
Dose	1 teaspoon per cup
	Tincture 4ml, 1-3 times daily
Constituents	Volatile oil, coumarins, bitters, tannins, silica, flavonoids, glycosides, polysaccharides
Primary action	Astringent
Secondary actions	Liver tonic
	Diuretic
How it works	Agrimony contains tannins which astringe – That is, they draw together tissues, so it benefits an inflamed digestive and urinary tract. Its bitters stimulate digestion and liver functions, which helps the process of detoxification. Coumarins regulate acidity and relax muscles, flavone glycosides promote diuresis and may increase the activity of the hormonal system by

stimulating hormone producing cells. The volatile oil gives it a pleasant taste and may contribute an anti-viral effect. It is traditionally used as a spring tonic.

Betony

(see Nervous restoratives)

Damiana

Latin name	Turnera diffusa
Origin	South America
Part used	Leaf
Dose	1 teaspoon per cup,
	Tincture 4ml, 1-3 times daily
Constituents	Volatile oil (including thymol, arbutin), bitters, alkaloids, flavonoids, cyanogenic glycosides
Primary actions	Tonic
	Anti-depressant
Secondary actions	Anti-infective
	Diuretic
How it works	Damiana's volatile oil has lots of strongly anti-bacterial components, including arbutin, which is known to survive into the urinary tract where it relieves infections. Arbutin and flavonoids create the diuretic effect – increasing the elimination of water. The bitters increase digestive action and cyanogenic glycosides are mildly relaxing. It is thought that the flavonoids and alkaloids

are responsilble for the tonic effect on the
male hormonal system. Damiana is used as
an anti-depressant tonic for both sexes but is
primarily thought of as a 'gentleman's tonic'.

Growing guide   Not grown in Britain to date.

Dandelion

Latin name   Taraxacum officinalis
Origin   Europe
Part used   Root and leaf
Dose   1 teaspoon per cup
    Tincture 4ml, 1-3 times daily
Constituents   Bitters, sterols, inulin, polysaccharides,
    tannins, phenols, minerals, vitamins
Primary action   Tonic
Secondary action   Diuretic
How it works   Bitters and sterols in both leaf and root
    stimulate the liver, helping it to detoxify the
    body and improving digestion. Dandelion is
    also known for its gentle relief of
    constipation. The leaf is rich in potassium,
    which offsets losses due to extra elimination
    of water caused by its polysaccharides and
    inulin. Phenols are also diuretic and mildly
    antiseptic, having an anti-bacterial effect in
    the gut and urinary system. Dandelion is a
    general physical tonic. The root is a pleasant
    alternative to coffee.
Growing guide   Dandelion seeds itself everywhere. It is well
    worth growing as a salad leaf. The root

should be chopped before drying as it breaks
household implements when dry!

Poplar

Latin name	Populus tremuloides (also Populus alba, Populus nigra)
Origin	Europe and America
Part used	Bark
Dose	1 teaspoon per cup, Tincture 4ml, 1-3 times daily
Constituents	Populin, salicin, salicylic acid, tannins, phenols
Primary actions	Anti-inflammatory Tonic
Secondary actions	Diuretic Relieves fever
How it works	Salicin and salicylic acid relieve inflammation and pain by inhibiting production of inflammatory chemical messangers. Salicylic acid is also noted for relieving high temperatures by altering the body thermostat in the hypothalamus. It is mildly bitter, so improves digestive secretions which can increase energy extraction from foods. Its phenols are antiseptic in the urinary system and its tannins help to reduce inflammation and bacterial population in the digestive tract. Poplar used to be commonly used in convalescence. Ideal for post-viral depressive states in conjunction with others.

Growing guide Large tree, useful for masking traffic noise due to the constant rustling of its leaves. It will tolerate damp clay soils.

Rosemary

Latin name	Rosemarinus officinalis
Origin	Europe
Part used	Leaf
Dose	1 teaspoon per cup
	Tincture 4ml, 1-3 times daily
Constituents	Volatile oil, flavonoids, tannins, bitters, phenols, resins
Primary actions	Tonic
	Relaxant
Secondary actions	Anti-spasmodic
	Circulatory tonic
How it works	Rosemary's volatile oil stimulates the skin, raising circulation there and stimulating the brain via the sense of smell and the blood stream. Unlike other stimulants, it does not increase the heart rate. It is said that volatile oils such as those in rosemary can actually penetrate the brain, causing a mild stimulant effect. This may account for rosemary's long history of being 'the herb for remembrance'. Its bitters stimulate digestion, hence their popular association with fatty meats such as lamb. Flavonoids help to strengthen blood vessel walls and phenols are mildly antiseptic in the gut, reducing bacterial ferment and

relieving wind. Together with an anti-spasmodic action this is known as the carminative effect. The phenols also help to relieve dandruff and the mild stimulant effect on the scalp helps to improve hair condition.

Growing guide   Rosemary is an evergreen and easy to propagate by cuttings, but it dislikes cold wind, so if exposed will lose leaves and turn brown.

Growing and making your own herbal remedies

You can prepare herbs in a wide variety of ways to relieve anxiety and stress.

Types of herbal preparation

Oral remedies

Oral remedies are swallowed in measured doses. They include:

- teas
- tinctures
- syrups
- pills.

Topical remedies

Topical remedies are applied to the skin and include:

- creams
- oils
- baths
- plasters and poultices.

Oral remedies

Teas or tisanes

Teas, also called tisanes, can be made directly from dried herbs.

- Leaves and flowers require five minutes steeping in freshly boiled water. Always place a saucer or cover on the cup to keep in valuable aromatic ingredients. This is known as an **infusion**.
- Roots, barks, seeds and berries need boiling for five minutes in a covered pan. This is called a **decoction**.

The usual dose is one rounded teaspoon per cup (about 4g to 165ml). Regular use means one or two cups per day for several weeks. Infusions and decoctions can be drunk cold, and any flavouring can be added after steeping or boiling.

- To make an infusion steep cut leaf or flower for 5-10 minutes in boiling water.
- To make a decoction boil cut root or bark for 5-10 minutes on the stove.

Many people ask if the dosage of dried herbs should be different from fresh herbs. As the loss of chemicals in drying may balance the greater concentration due to loss of water, it is best to simply use the same amounts whether fresh or dry. Some herbs such as lemon balm, chamomile and basil taste better when fresh and are slightly more effective, but most herbs keep their medicinal qualities very well if dried carefully. Roots and barks often improve their taste with drying as they lose their acrid components and become sweeter.

Measurements
1ml = 1g
1 teaspoon = 5ml
1cup = 165ml
Tinctures are usually 1: 5, or one part herb to five parts alcoholic liquid.

Doses for adults
Adults will usually require one to three cups a day of herbal teas (whether infused or decocted), using one teaspoon of herb per cup.

Adult doses of tincture vary according to the herbs used in them. Usually half a teaspoon of single herb tinctures, three times daily, is required. With great care you can get 80 drops onto a 5ml teaspoon, so you can work out your dose that way too, and use the formula given below to calculate a child's dose. The amount of alcohol in one teaspoon of tincture is very small, but you can add the remedy to hot water and allow some of the alcohol to evaporate if you wish. Elderly people may require different doses, as body weight falls or if digestion isn't as good. One should start with a lower dose and work up if required.

Doses for children
Children require smaller doses. There are some formulae

which can be used, based on a child's age. For example, divide the child's age by twenty, to give the proportion of an adult dose, i.e. 6 (years) divided by 20 = 3/10 adult dose. You also have to take into account the child's body weight, giving less if a child is underweight for his/her age.

Common doses for teas are: a tablespoon of tea to a child under 5, half a cup for a child from 5 to 10 years and a full cup from 11 years onwards. Beatrice Potter seems to agree, as Peter Rabbit was given a large spoonful of chamomile tea after he had over-eaten in Mr McGregor's garden!

Making your own formula

You can combine herbs in tincture or tea form to obtain a mixture of effects which will suit your individual needs. Start by choosing the actions that you want – for example relaxant, pain relieving, hormonal, and look for herbs which provide them. It is best to include no more than three or four herbs in one mixture, and with careful selection you can choose herbs with more than one action to match your requirements.

If you are using dried or fresh herbs to make teas, you should choose herbs which require the same sort of preparation (remember that roots, barks and seeds need boiling, leaves and flowers need infusing). You will only need one teaspoon of your mix because herbs act synergistically as you have learnt already.

Tinctures

These have become very popular in Britain, both among herbalists and consumers. They are made by soaking herbal material, finely chopped, in an alcoholic liquid about 70% proof. This could be brandy or vodka. Generally, you use one part herb to five parts liquid, so 100g to 500ml. Chop the herbs as finely as possible and cover with the alcohol. Turn, shake or stir every day for ten days. This is to ensure that every particle of herb is in contact with alcohol, otherwise moulds may develop. After ten days, strain and squeeze out the remaining 'marc' through a clean piece of material. Keep the tincture you have made in a dry bottle with a tight stopper.

This can be used in place of herbal tea. Each teaspoon of tincture generally gives the effect of a small cup of tea. Sometimes herbal constituents are extracted better by alcohol, so it is a useful way of preserving herbs. In the past, wines and vinegars were used. Their trace is found in the nursery rhyme Jack and Jill where Old Dame Dob did mend Jack's nob with vinegar and brown paper.

Tincture of Lemon Balm
100g lemon balm
500ml vodka or brandy

Chop herbs finely, cover with alcohol, shake or stir daily for ten days, strain and bottle.

It is obvious that these are much bigger doses than is

often suggested on over-the-counter tincture bottles, where the manufacturer is more concerned with keeping the price and profit margin at an attractive level. Tinctures are more expensive than teas, and you should expect to pay between £3 and £5 for a week's supply.

Herbal syrups

Herbs can be preserved in syrup but they are quite difficult to make as the proportion of sugar to herbal material is crucial. They frequently go mouldy, however carefully you measure. There are two methods, the first is the simplest but only keeps for a few days.

Syrup recipe 1

Place chopped herb and sugar in 1cm layers in a clean, dry jar, finishing with a sugar layer. Leave for one day. You will find a syrup has formed. You can shake the jar gently once a day until all the sugar has turned into syrup. This may take three days but you can use the product immediately.

Syrup recipe 2

Soak 4g of herb, finely chopped, in 56ml water for 12 hours. Strain and squeeze out the herbs. There should be about 45ml liquid. Add 90g sugar, stir over heat until dissolved, boil briefly, strain through a filter paper or cloth. You should have about 100ml syrup. This must be kept in a well stoppered bottle in a cool, dry, dark cupboard. The dose would usually be 1 teaspoon at a time for children, and a dessertspoon from 11 years onwards.

Pills

These come in two main varieties: pills and capsules. In both cases, powdered herbs are used. Capsules are usually made of gelatine, although vegetarian ones can be obtained. Most are of a standard size, containing about 2g of herb. You can buy herbs ready powdered and fill your own capsules by hand. It's a very sneezy, time consuming business! Tablets are made by pressing powdered herbs into the required shape. You will need to add ingredients to make the dough stick together and the tablets hold their shape. Manufacturers usually use vegetable gums, but quite satisfactory tablets can be made at home using honey and arrowroot as binders. Pills can either be pinched off and rolled between the fingers or tablets cut by hand from dough rolled with a pin.

Buckwheat pills

2 tablespoons buckwheat flour
1 tablespoon Arrowroot powder
4 teaspoons runny honey

Knead all ingredients together. Add more honey if required to achieve a malleable paste. Dust board with arrowroot, roll out, cut to shape, dry on paper overnight.

Topical remedies

There are several forms in which herbs can be applied to the outside of your body. This is known as topical application. You need to remember a little bit about skin to understand how herbs reach their target when used in this way.

The skin

Skin has several layers designed to keep water in (you suffer dehydration quickly if large areas of skin are broken) but allow moisture out when required to cool the body down by evaporation. It is covered with a cornified layer (dead cells) and wax. Blood vessels are very close to the surface, and they dilate when we are hot, to allow heat out by convection. They also dilate when we are emotionally stressed, so we flush with anger, embarassment, or affection. These blood vessels can constrict to conserve heat, and sometimes when we are very angry or upset we become paler than our usual colour.

Fat underneath the skin keeps heat in by insulation and protects some areas from pressure (famously the bum!). Muscle is found underneath linings below the fatty layer. If you want to reach muscles, your topical applications must somehow get through the wax, cornified layer, fat and muscle linings first. Oily preparations do penetrate through these layers to some extent.

One way of increasing penetration is to soak the skin in water for a while. This can be done in the bath, in a steam room, or on small areas with a poultice or plaster. Belladonna plasters for back pain could still be bought in the chemist's until a few years ago. Most people have heard of anti-smoking and hormone patches. These use the same principle. Back to Old Dame Dob and her vinegar on brown paper!

Four ways of increasing absorption through the skin:

- bath
- steam
- poultice
- plaster.

Creams

Creams are more complicated to make. It would be easier to choose a favourite bland cream over the counter and add aromatic oils or tinctures as you wish. If you want to try a cream, try the following recipe.

Rosemary cream

8 parts oil
1 part beeswax
a few drops essential oil

Gently heat oil and beeswax together in a bowl, set in a pan of water. When wax has melted, add essential oil and pour into pots immediately.

Greasy ointments like this are generally not considered to be good for skin conditions such as eczema, where they inhibit healing and trap heat, but they are suitable for applying as muscle and joint rubs. Their advantage over liquid preparations is that they don't drip on your carpet.

Massage oils

This option is useful if you want to use herbs from your garden. Simply pick a handful of fresh herbs, chop finely and cover loosely with any oil – almond, olive or even sunflower oil. Place the bowl of oil and herbs in a pan of water and put the lid on. Heat until simmering and leave on the lowest possible heat for 1-2 hours. A slow-pot can give ideal conditions for making infused oils as it maintains a constant very low simmering temperature. Spices can also be infused in vegetable oils.

There are many essential oils available now which save you the time involved in infusing plants in oil. The easiest way to apply these is in a carrier oil such as olive, almond or coconut. A few drops to a tablespoon will suffice. You can add a dash of chilli or ginger! Massaging increases blood flow to muscles and breaks down the tension in them. Rubbing creams and oils into small joints, such as fingers and toes, can give quite effective pain relief, and is particularly useful where the patient is unable to take any oral medication.

Baths

Essential oils can be added to the bath. Use a teaspoon of unscented bubble bath, or a tablespoon of milk to act as a dispersant. Relaxing bath salts are based on the same principle and available commercially, although they don't smell as nice as genuine essential oils. The relaxing effect is limited, but a helpful contribution, especially at night before bed, and there are no side-effects.

Plasters and poultices

These are used to apply steady heat or continued absorption of pain relieving or relaxing constituents to joints or muscles.

Plasters are made by melting one part of beeswax and two parts of vegetable oil, adding tincture or essential oil at the last minute. Soak a suitable sized cloth in the mix and spread out on a tray to cool and firm up. Apply to the body and cover in plastic or cling film (or paper!) and tie on with a bandage or some tight garment. The most common use is application to chest, back, abdomen and forehead. You could add a hot water bottle or hot towel wrap for extra comfort.

Poultices are similar to plasters, but consist of a 1cm thick layer of fresh or macerated herbs applied to the skin and covered with a piece of material. This was the earlier form of a plaster, but can still be immediate and effective.

Choosing herbs

Identifying herbs in the wild

It is important first of all to know that you have the right plant. Some botanical families include poisonous and edible plants which look very similar and can only be distinguished from each other by fine botanical detail, like hemlock and valerian, which have subtle differences in stem and flower colouring. You could buy a field botany guide, as identification of plants is a great hobby, but it would be wiser not to select your remedies from the wild if you are a complete beginner.

Fortunately many of the most important medicinal herbs are garden favourites such as thyme, sage, rosemary, lemon balm and peppermint. Most people recognise them and they are pretty unmistakeable. Even where there are different varieties such as the thymes and mints, they have the same aroma and characteristics. It is better to choose the original sort for medicinal purposes rather than a variety because it may be a more reliable source of the chemicals that you need for your remedy.

Choosing herbs

There is a system of naming plants which gives each one two Latin names – the family name comes first and has a capital letter, the individual name comes second written in lower case. The meaning is reversed in Latin, for example *Thymus vulgaris* means common thyme. This is the one you would use for cough medicine. Other types, such as *Thymus aureus*, (golden thyme) or *Thymus serpillus* (creeping thyme) will do no harm, but they don't have as much aroma – in fact they put most of their energy into looking pretty! The same can be said for the many lovely varieties of achillea – a cottage garden flower related to yarrow (*Achillea officinalis*) The word *officinalis* in a plant's name means it was known to be used medicinally in the seventeenth century or before. You will need to specify both names when you are buying seeds or plants from nurseries. Addresses of reliable firms are given on page 122.

Growing herbs

Many of the herbs mentioned in this book can be grown in British gardens, some can be grown in pots or on window ledges. Growing herbs is a very relaxing and rewarding hobby. Although most aromatic herbs originate in the warm Mediterranean countries, they will do fine in a sunny spot in any garden soil, even on London clay. They do prefer well drained (slightly dry) soil, so adding grit and compost will help them along.

   If you are growing from seed you will need to start them off in pots first on a window ledge or in a greenhouse. To sow seeds really successfully, you should buy John Innes compost number 1. This contains lots of sand and fine grit, so that water runs through quickly and the seed doesn't sit in its own tiny puddle of water, which causes a fungal growth gardeners call damping off.

When you have a small stem with two leaves, pull it up gently and plant in a pot with John Innes number 2 compost. This has more soil, so that fine roots can spread and take in water – it also contains a little more nutrient to feed the growing plant. When your plant is about 10 cm tall or has a few branches, it's time to plant it in a sunny spot or container, using John Innes number 3. John Innes is a type of compost, not a brand name, so you can ask for it at any garden nursery.

Planting out

Locate your herbs in the south west corner of your garden if possible. Herbs don't need feeding or watering once they have extended their roots into the garden soil (after about a week) but containers will need to be watered as they dry out continually. You can even grow herbs in hanging baskets. You can use multi-purpose compost, but you run a much greater risk of damping-off and losing seed before they even grow, which can mean a whole growing year lost. If your plants don't succeed in one spot in your garden, move them! Just dig up enough soil around the plant to ensure minimum root disturbance and put them in somewhere else. Experiment to see what works. There are plenty of herbs to choose from, so find one that suits your garden or space.

- choose a sunny spot
- add grit to improve drainage
- start tender plants under glass
- water pots and baskets daily
- move plants if they aren't happy.

Choosing the right part of the plant

It is important to know which part of the plant you need if you are going to make your own herbal remedies. Flowers, leaves, roots, bark and berries are commonly used but sometimes one part of a plant is edible whereas another part is poisonous. We eat the tuberous root of the potato but avoid the berries and we eat rhubarb stems but not the leaves. Comfrey root stores too many alkaloids which can damage the liver, whereas they are barely present in the leaf. It is common to find stems in with leaves in herbs sold over the counter, as it is difficult to separate them when preparing herbs on a large scale. If you are preparing your own, you should take the trouble to rub the leaves off the stems as your remedy will be stronger without this inert woody matter.

Harvesting herbs

Choosing the right time to harvest is also important. It helps you to get the best quality of herbs in terms of the chemical constituents.

- Leaves are picked just before flowers develop.

- Flowers are picked as they come out.
- Berries as they become fully ripe, while they are still smooth and shiny.
- Bark and stem is stripped in the late spring from new branches.
- Roots are dug up in early autumn before the first frosts. Pick on a dry day, and scrub roots immediately after digging.

Storing herbs

Most plants can be used fresh, but it is more convenient to dry them for use all the year round. The rules for drying herbs are:

- as cool, fast, dark and dry as possible, with as much air circulating around the individual herbs as can be allowed.

The best way for home preservation is to hang up small bunches of herbs, loosely tied, in a dark room or shed. A washing-line strung across the attic is ideal. Hanging up in the kitchen will cause most of the colour and aroma to be lost before they dry.

Large roots should be chopped before drying, as they will prove too tough for the knife otherwise. They can be spread out in a single layer on newspapers. The newspapers should be changed when they feel very damp.

Herbal material is ready to store when it is cracking dry.

This is a matter of experience. Usually leaves will simply not leave their stems until they are thoroughly dry. Roots should snap briskly or fail to bend under pressure. Berries usually give a little under thumb pressure. They are slow to dry – moulds develop if there is too much moisture so gentle heat (airing cupboard level) is helpful. When thoroughly dry herbs should be stored in cool, dark ,dry, airless conditions because sunlight destroys colour, air removes flavour and water causes moulds. Tin boxes are ideal, however plastic tubs and glass jars are OK provided they are kept in a cupboard.

- Hang leaves on branches upside down.
- Spread roots out in a single layer.
- Dry as fast as possible in a cool, dark, airy place.
- Ready when cracking dry.
- Keep in cool, dark, dry, airless conditions.

∼ 6 ∼

Using nutrition to improve stress resistance

Achieving a balanced diet

Stressed people often have poor diets. That doesn't mean that diet can cause or cure anxiety and tension, but there are many ways in which you can improve your resistance to stress.

A healthy diet

The main aim of a healthy diet is to satisfy the need for energy, growth, repair and elimination.

A therapeutic diet

A therapeutic diet is one that addresses the needs of people with a particular complaint, for example gluten free diets for coeliac disease, sugar-free diets for diabetes and so on.

Anxious, tense and depressed people should aim at a general healthy diet with special attention to:

- avoiding stimulants
- maintaining energy levels
- obtaining high nutrient content.

Daily requirements for nutrients

In Britain research into food was started during World War II and was continued by the Ministry of Agriculture and Fisheries with help from the Medical Research Council. They produced guidelines on what people need to eat to keep them healthy and prevent deficiencies. These are called the **minimum daily requirements** and they cover the main nutrients needed by the human body. In America USDA (the United States Department of Agriculture) funds a similar programme, and its books are widely used in Britain.

It is a mistake to look at single nutrients as being a cure for specific conditions, as almost all body processes require a broad range of nutrients to keep them running smoothly. All human cells need sugar as a fuel to perform their vital functions. Muscles use sugar for fuel as well as calcium and potassium to contract and relax. Salt (sodium) plays an essential role in getting calcium into muscle fibre cells and potassium is vital to maintain the correct amount of salt in the body. All these processes are dependent on each other and on a balanced state of nutrients in the body. This is the state of health which the herbalist tries to restore with herbal medicines and wholistic dietary advice.

It is usual to divide food up into seven different categories and we should aim to eat something in each category every day.

You could use these categories to design a food diary or plan your eating for a week.

- Protein – cheese, meat, beans, nuts, fish
- Starch – bread, potatoes, pasta, roots, rice, grains
- Vitamin A – green, orange and yellow vegetables
- Vitamin B – meat, wholegrains
- Vitamin C – fresh fruit and green vegetables
- Vitamin D – fish oil and sunlight
- Vitamin E – wholegrains and seeds
- Vitamin P – also known as bioflavonoids – fresh fruit and vegetables
- Minerals – calcium, potassium, sodium, magnesium, zinc, phosphorus, found in vegetable and animal foods
- Trace Elements – cobalt, copper etc, found in vegetable and animal foods
- Fibre – indigestible parts of vegetables and grains
- Fat – butter, cooking oil, margarine.

Daily requirements for nutrients vary according to age and occupation (whether you have an active or sedentary job). Here we have taken the figures for sedentary workers. You can use these tables to understand information given on labelling of supplements

- 1mg = one thousandth of 1g , 1µg = 1 millionth of 1g

	Men 35-64	Women 18-54
kcals	2,400	2,150
protein	60g	54g
calcium	500mg	500mg
iron	10mg	12mg
vitamin A	750µg	750µg
thiamin (vitamin B₁)	1mg	.8mg
riboflavin (vitamin B₂)	1.6mg	1.3mg
niacin (vitamin B)	18mg	15mg
vitamin C	30mg	30mg
vitamin D	10µg if no sunlight available	10µg if no sunlight available

Women's needs vary to a greater extent than men's because of changes taking place during pregnancy, breastfeeding, the monthly menstrual cycle and menopause. British guidelines suggest that women over 55 take fewer calories (1,900kcals) and less iron (10mg) daily. The lower iron intake is suggested because there will be no monthly losses due to menstruation and the smaller calorie intake reflects metabolic changes after the menopause.

American researchers give us figures for some of the other vital nutrients which apply to both men and women.

vitamin K	70-140µg
biotin (vitamin B)	100-200µg
pantothenin (vitamin B)	4-7mg
potassium	1,875-562 mg
phosphorus	700-800mg
sodium	1,100-3,300
chloride	1,700-5,100

Canadian guidelines complete the picture, with daily requirements for men and women between 25 and 49 and recommendations for the over 50s (blank means no change).

	Men	(over 50)	Women	(over 50)
vitamin E	9mg	7mg	6mg	
folacin (vitamin B)	220µg		175µg	190µg
pyridoxine (vitamin B_{12})	2µg		2µg	
magnesium	250mg		200mg	210mg
calcium	800mg		700mg	800mg
iodine	160µg		160µg	
zinc	9mg		8mg	

It is interesting to note that Canadian researchers think we need a lot more daily calcium than do their British counterparts. This is because they recommend a much higher protein intake which causes greater loss of calcium from the body. You may need to take this into account when you are looking at labels on vitamin and mineral supplements.

Other minerals considered essential for daily nutrition are chromium, selenium, molybdenum, copper, manganese and fluoride. The intakes for these are generally very small figures – from .2 to .5µg. These are called trace elements.

The guidelines presented above are based on the amounts needed to stop you developing a deficiency condition, such as scurvy which develops when you don't get enough vitamin C. Some nutritionists think you need more than these if you have certain diseases, but this is a very undefined area, with lots of claims motivated by the desire to sell products. General health is achieved by eating a balance of all necessary nutrients, which will help the body grow and repair itself, two vital processes for withstanding the effects of stress.

Relieving anxiety and tension through diet

Many British people rely on tea and coffee for their daily intake of liquid, often drinking eight or more cups daily. These drinks contain caffeine, which is a very potent sympathetic stimulant. It makes the heart beat faster, causes sweating and eventually constriction of blood vessels in the skin. Other effects of caffeine include tremors, palpitations, raised blood pressure and cholesterol.

Caffeine content of drinks	
1 cup brewed coffee	80mg
1 cup instant coffee	60mg
1 cup tea	50mg
1 cup green tea	30mg
1 (12oz) can cola	32-65mg (depends on brand)
1 cup cocoa	6-42mg (depends on brand)

Some of these drinks also contain chemicals which affect our digestion and well-being. Coffee contains chemicals which irritate the stomach and gut lining, often causing loose bowel movements and acid indigestion. Tea contains tannins, which prevent the absorption of minerals and vitamins when ingested together and increased acidity when drunk on its own (but it contains relaxing chemicals such as theobromine as well). It is interesting to see that many brands of cola contain as much caffeine as a cup of instant coffee and more than a cup of tea. They also contain large amounts of 'hidden' sugar which aggravates obesity and acids which destroy tooth enamel.

When to drink tea and coffee

It would seem that tea is best drunk in the afternoon, with a piece of fruit cake for its reviving and relaxing qualities, whereas coffee is best suited to after a main meal, when it helps digestion and food minimises its effect on the stomach. Cola was originally a stamina drink (the addictive stimulant coca was removed some time ago although the name remains) made from coca leaves. It could be useful for dancing 'til dawn.

Regular between-meals use of stimulant drinks such as coffee mobilises fats into the bloodstream for energy use but also stimulates insulin cells in the pancreas. This means that sugar is removed from the bloodstream quite quickly and a 'hungry low' follows, which is only satisfied by consumption of quickly absorbed carbohydrate. These snacks cause a feeling of fullness which then reduces the appetite for more nutritious food at main mealtimes.

Snacks and diabetes

Some researchers think that taking too many stimulant drinks followed by carbohydrate snacks can lead to failure of the pancreatic response, as repeated demands are made for insulin in high quantities. Stress reactions also increase insulin response, so a combination of these factors may be involved in the development of diabetes. Certainly the low blood sugar episodes, which this pattern of eating may favour, cause irritability, lack of concentration, headaches and nausea. Many people experience periods of this sort of feeling daily and reach for a chocolate snack, which perpetuates the problem.

Stress eating

There is evidence that, under the influence of the stress hormone – adrenaline, glucose (simple sugar) is drawn from the body's stores ready to be used by muscles for fuel. If you fail to burn this up in exercise it is stored as fat but the body now experiences low blood sugar and you are driven to eat earlier, despite the calories not having left your body as energy. This cycle is reinforced by regular stimulant drinks which enhance adrenaline effects.

Caffeine-free alternatives

There are many delicious alternatives to caffeine-rich drinks. Here is a list of tried and tested favourites. Methods for preparing teas are simple (see Chapter 5). Most of them can be drunk cold as well as hot. Try:

- hibiscus and orange peel
- orange peel and cinnamon
- hibiscus and dried apple
- lemon peel and ginger
- orange blossom and vanilla.

Most of the relaxing herbs make delicious teas, especially jasmine, peppermint, spearmint, lemon balm, limeflowers, lemon verbena and passionflower. Many people love chamomile, it is exquisite when made from fresh flowers, but sometimes a little bitter when brewed too long from dried flowers. Mate tea is a South American relative of China tea and has about the same amount of caffeine as green tea.

If you prefer milky drinks you can try:

- malted milk (traditional brand Horlicks, or make your own)
- cocoa (see note below)
- carob
- Barley Cup (and other commercially roasted grain drinks)
- dandelion
- chicory.

The last two are often combined for a fairly convincing coffee substitute. The amount of caffeine in a cup of cocoa is usually quite low.

Bedtime drinks

Milky drinks with sugar or malt are especially useful at bedtime, as protein (in milk) contains tryptophan, which is converted to serotonin and appears to aid sleep. It seems that tryptophan cannot enter the brain unless it is accompanied by carbohydrate, which causes insulin to be released and clear competing proteins from the pathways. The sugars in bedtime drinks serve this purpose, and they are able to release tryptophan from earlier protein intake. Starchy milk dishes such as rice, semolina, tapioca and macaroni have the same effect. No wonder we fall asleep after a traditional British Sunday lunch! Vegans can make these drinks with soya, as there is just a little less tryptophan in soya milk than in cow's milk.

Carbohydrates and energy

Carbohydrate is another name for starch. It can be divided into two groups:

- Refined carbohydrate contains no fibre. This group includes sugar, white bread, rice and pasta.
- Complex carbohydrate is attached to fibre. This group includes wholemeal bread, brown rice and pasta, vegetables, fruits and pulses (beans and lentils).

In addition fibre can be divided into two groups:

- Soluble fibre. This includes gums and pectin found in fruits.
- Insoluble fibre. This includes bran and cellulose found in grains and pulses.

You have read how refined carbohydrate can make high demands on the pancreas and displace more nutritious food from your daily diet. Eating complex carbohydrate can have a more beneficial effect on your health and energy. It slows the entry of sugar into the bloodstream as it has to be extracted from its complex package first. Fibre is filling but non calorific, it reduces the amount you need to be satisfied, so you are getting less calories per slice if you make cakes and bread with wholemeal flour instead of white. If you add dried fruits to white bread, you increase fibre and sweetness without a large increase in calories. Teabread (barabrith,teacake) is a great breakfast slice, giving you energy, minerals, vitamins and fibre!

Eating regular meals

Eating for energy means eating regularly and balancing your meals. Most people need three or four meals daily, with enough energy content and nutrients to provide for the daily needs. The body needs new energy supplies roughly every four hours and doesn't function as well on one meal a day. Without instantly available energy

concentration decreases, physical fatigue is felt and
irritability sets in.

Eating breakfast

Breakfast is an essential meal if you are to give your best
in the morning. It is a difficult meal to eat for many
people who have to get up early and commute to work.
Those who are retired will often find that they eat
breakfast an hour or so after rising. It might be easier to
take breakfast with you to work. All you need is a tub of
cereal at work and a leakproof container to carry your
choice of milk. Cereal-based breakfasts seem the easiest
way to obtain a balanced mix of nutrients, liquid and
starch. If you use yoghurt on your cereal instead of milk
you increase your protein intake, and yoghurt is easier to
transport.

Work-place microwaves are common now and make
porridge – the queen of breakfast cereals – an easy
possibility. Try adding mixed fruits to make a traditional
dish called frumenty. Powdered cinnamon on top turns
this nutritious cereal into a gourmet experience!

Which vitamins and minerals are good for stress?

There aren't any specific vitamins or minerals which
relieve stress, anxiety or tension. Vitamins act

synergistically, like plant chemicals, to help the body deal with stress. It is possible that an anxious person might have a faster pulse rate and that their metabolism might speed up, so that nutrients are used up more quickly. This produces a greater demand for all nutrients, not just one or two.

Eating a balanced diet (outlined earlier in this chapter) which is rich in plant foods is probably the best thing you can do to protect your body from the effects of stress. It may also be useful to focus on particular essential nutrients which may be lacking in a busy person's daily diet.

Vitamin C

Vitamin C, chemical name ascorbic acid, is involved in all energy and repair processes in the body, as well as disease resistance. It is not stored in the body, so you must take some every day. In nature this vitamin is usually found with a group of chemicals called bioflavonoids (sometimes referred to as Vitamin P). Vitamin P helps to protect the blood vessels from damage and makes them more elastic. This means they will be more able to withstand changes caused by stress and illness.

Recommended intake of Vitamin C is 30mg in Britain, 60mg in America. British figures are, as explained before, based on the amounts needed to prevent deficiency diseases. American and Canadian figures are higher, in line with all their other recommendations.

Vitamin C content of foods

		% of daily requirement
1 cup orange juice	124mg	200%
$1/2$ Canteloupe melon	113mg	188%
1 cup cooked broccoli	98mg	163%
1 green pepper	95mg	158%
1 orange	70mg	116%
1 cup cooked cauliflower	69mg	115%
1 cup parsley	54mg	90%
raw cabbage	33mg	55%
baked potato	26mg	34%

You should cut the vegetables just before using and cook them conservatively – that is, using just enough water to cover – boil the kettle first and add to vegetables. Boil until just tender, use the water in gravy. This method conserves the vitamin C, which is lost to heat, air and water. Steaming vegetables is even better, but you will need to add salt at the table. Frozen vegetables retain some of their vitamin content. Supermarket vegetables may have lost some vitamins in transport. The best vitamin content is obtained by growing your own and picking just before eating.

Gardening is also very good for reducing stress!

B vitamins

These are necessary for every process in the body, including nerve transmission and protein building, as they are part of the process which turns sugar into fuel which every cell in the body needs to carry on its work. This affects nerve transmission, building structures such as muscle and bone, as well as making new 'fabrics' such as skin and mucous membranes. It is worth looking at these vitamins for energy and health, especially as some researchers think many people are deficient in them.

Thiamin
Vitamin B1, daily requirement 1 5mg

Food	Amount per 100g	Normal portion	% daily requirement
brewers' yeast	15.6mg	10g	100%
sunflower seeds	2mg	50g	66%
pork	1mg	100g	66%
green peas	.5mg	50g	16%
wheatgerm	2g	10g	13%
wholewheat bread	.34mg	25g	5%

Tea contains a small amount of thiamin, one cup is equivalent to a slice of wholemeal bread, but because of the quantities drunk in Britain it is a significant contributor to our thiamin intake.

Riboflavin
Vitamin B^2, daily requirement 1.2mg

Food	Amount per 100g	Normal portion	% of daily requirement
liver	4.6mg	100g	400%
almonds	.7mg	50g	29%
Marmite	11mg	3g	27%
beefsteak	.23mg	100g	19%
milk	.17mg	100ml	14%

Tea also contains a small amount of riboflavin and because of the amount we drink this may be a significant contributor to our daily need.

Niacin
Vitamin B^3, daily requirement 13g

Food	Amount per 100g	Normal portion	% daily requirement
tuna	15.5mg	100g	119%
peanuts	14.3mg	50g	111%
liver	14.4mg	100g	111%
chicken	5.9mg	100g	45%
brewers' yeast	39mg	10g	29%
mushrooms	4.4mg	50g	16%

Tea also contains good amounts of niacin, and can make an important contribution to our daily need. Niacin can be made in the body from tryptophan, which is present in cheese, fish, eggs and meat, with small amounts in bread, potatoes, brown rice and wheatgerm.

Folacin
Vitamin B⁴, daily requirement 165 µg

Food	Amount per 100g	Normal portion	% daily requirement
brewers' yeast	3912µg	10g	236%
spinach	467µg	50g	141%
sunflower seeds	236µg	50g	71%
haricot beans	56.8µg	75g	25%
broccoli	68.5µg	50g	20%
wheatgerm	82µg	50g	24%

Dandelion leaf contains the same amount per 100g as wheatgerm.

Pyridoxine
Vitamin B⁶, daily requirement .2mg

Food	Amount per 100g	Normal portion	% daily requirement
salmon	.8mg	100g	40%
sunflower seeds	1.2mg	50g	30%
brewers' yeast	5mg	10g	25%
banana	.51mg	75g	19%
baked potato	.25mg	150g	18%
beefsteak	.27mg	100g	13%

Carob flour is reported to have very large amounts of B⁶

but the data is not confirmed.

Biotin and Pantothenic acid

These are also B vitamins, but they are not normally included in detailed tables because they occur in almost all foods and deficiencies are unknown.

Cobalamine

Vitamin B12, daily requirement 2-3µg

The trace of vitamin B12 in food is so small that no detailed figures are available. It was once thought that you could only obtain this essential vitamin from animal foods, but recent research shows it to be present in pulses, such as mung beans, peas, alfalfa and soya beans. Comfrey leaf and whole wheat are also thought to provide useful amounts, though comfrey is usually taken in short courses of eight weeks, with breaks between, as its alkaloids can accumulate in the liver. Consult a medical herbalist for more information on this.

How do you ensure the right amount of B vitamins in your diet?

You should eat enough from each group to supply your daily requirement. B vitamins are water soluble so you should use the minimum water to cook your foods, and keep the water to make sauce or gravy. The figures presented here give fairly large portions for meat and small for nuts or vegetables. This is based on general eating habits as represented in statistics. You can do the reverse, vegetarians and vegans would do this anyway. You must always aim to take a balance of B vitamins, as excesses or deficiencies in one can disturb the effect of the others.

How to increase B vitamins in your diet

Increases in this list refer to normal portions in the tables above.

- add brewers' yeast to drinks, soups and sauces
- eat more liver and flavour it with tomato or orange
- add wheatgerm to your breakfast cereal
- add sunflower seeds to breads, cakes, salads and snacks
- add mushrooms to meat dishes
- try mushrooms on toast, in soup, in deep pizzas
- eat oily fish regularly
- add peanuts to nut roasts and vegesausage mix
- use ground almonds to thicken sauce
- eat wholegrain bread made with yeast
- eat brown rice
- a nice cup of tea daily will add some B vitamins to your diet!

Finally, lots of studies show that people who eat a lot of green, leafy vegetables tend to suffer less from water retention and high blood pressure.

7

Case histories

The remedies described here were made up of one-to-five tincture (one part herbs to five parts alcohol, for example 100g herbs to 500ml vodka), equal amounts of each herb were used unless otherwise stated. The dose was 1 teaspoonful (5ml), three times daily.

Case 1 Depression, anxiety and cold sores

Miss S was a 30 year old residential social worker. Her job involved night-time supervision of teenagers in care homes, as well as working within a fractious and divided staff team. Miss S had suffered from depression since her teenage years, with one severe episode for which she spent time in hospital. Her main emotional symptoms were weepiness, loss of confidence and acute anxiety. Her physical symptoms included frequent headaches, constipation, tight feelings in the chest and very light periods. She sought a consultation initially for recurrent coldsores (herpes), which occurred in clusters around her nose and were particularly painful. They tended to erupt before periods but also before exams and interviews. This was a special problem, as she was trying to leave her stressful job and wanted to look her best for potential employers.

Miss S smoked heavily, twenty rollups per day, and took Amitryptiline daily, although she was in the process of reducing her dose of this anti-depressant.

The strategy

We decided to prioritise improving immunity and relieve the emotional tension which encouraged the herpes virus to replicate. As Miss S had reduced her current medicine to a quarter dose, we included a herbal anti-depressant.

The remedy

- Echinacea – immune stimulant.
- St John's wort – nervous restorative, anti-depressant.
- Vervein – anti-viral, nervous restorative, relaxant.
- Avena – nervous restorative, nutritive.

In addition marigold and echinacea tincture was applied topically as a healing, anti-viral immune stimulant.

The result

Only one herpes lesion occurred in the next month, after Miss S failed her driving test, but it resolved very quickly. In the second month of taking herbal medicine she experienced a more normal period and another small herpes attack. By the fourth month Miss S was experiencing 'the tingle' but had no full-blown attacks. She continued to take medicine for a year, feeling generally calmer, with very few cold sores.

Case 2 Fatigue and palpitations

Mrs M was a 40 year old nurse, now working in hospital administration after many years of nightshifts. She had two young children and had started her new job very recently. She sought a herbal consultation for heart palpitations. Recently she had been in hospital suffering from a severely disrupted heart rhythm known as ectopic tachycardia. She had been experiencing palpitations both before and since this episode. She described her symptoms as 'like missing a beat then feeling the heart thumping massively'. She also had a number of minor health problems, including repeated chest infections, water retention, facial acne and thrush. She had been prescribed progesterone treatment by her doctor, but she found that this gave her frequent headaches.

The strategy

Mrs M's main concerns were the palpitations and water retention, so the strategy concentrated on relieving tension and improving hormonal balance, but consideration was given to her recurrent infections as well.

The remedy

- Echinacea – immune stimulant.
- Chasteberry – hormonal balancer.
- Hops – relaxant, digestive tonic, hormonal agent.
- Rosemary – relaxant, circulatory tonic.

The result

The palpitations were greatly reduced by the end of one month and there was an improvement to premenstrual water retention over two months. Mrs M said that she felt more energetic although headaches still occurred at the time of her period. She continued to take herbal medicine for six months. Replacing rosemary with passionflower largely relieved the headaches.

Case 3 Muscular tension and digestive problems

Mr B was a 40 year old tiler, running his own business. He had a young family and some financial worries. He was suffering from chronic aching pains in his neck and head as well as heartburn, with acid regurgitation after alcoholic drinks, spicy and fatty foods. He was experiencing flatulence regularly and occasional mouth ulcers. He had recently become worried about loss of libido and sexual function. He drank about two litres of tea a day. His blood pressure was normal but his pulse was faster than average.

The strategy

We discussed his priorities and decided to soothe and tone his digestive system, relax his nerves and use tonics for his reproductive system.

The remedy

- Cramp Bark – muscle relaxant.
- Humulus – digestive tonic, relaxant.
- Damiana – tonic.
- Skullcap – relaxant.

The result

This brought immediate relief to digestive problems, so that Mr C could take spicy foods and moderate amounts of alcohol with no problem. He said that he had reduced his intake of tea, replacing it with water and herb teas. He reported a complete recovery of sexual function but his neck pain continued to be a problem. He was advised to develop an exercise strategy to relax and stretch muscles frequently while working, and we suggested visiting an osteopath to assess his muscle and joint condition more thoroughly.

Case 4 Nervous tension and arthritis

Mrs H was a retired company secretary, aged 74. She had been suffering from spinal arthritis for many years, probably due to damage occurring after TB which she contracted just after World War II. She had undergone several operations to correct a deviation of the spine and was distressed to find that arthritis was spreading to her wrists and knees, particularly as this affected her enjoyment of gardening. Her husband had died ten years before, followed by her closest friend four years later. She lived alone and was troubled by aggressive noisy neighbours. Mrs H had been suffering from insomnia for some years, for which she took Temazepam at night, but she didn't want to continue taking this regularly. She complained of having an 'overactive brain' and had difficulty keeping still, fidgeting and clenching her hands frequently. She had lost weight recently due to a series of digestive upsets, which she thought were infections.

In addition to these underlying stress factors, Mrs H's elderly dog was ill, and her house was undergoing major structural repairs.

The strategy

Mrs H's life had been extremely stressful for some time. She agreed wholeheartedly that this was the main source of her symptoms and so herbs were chosen to relax her mind, ease joint and muscle pain, and relieve digestive spasm as well as wind. Mrs H didn't feel confident about going out to yoga classes in the evening, but was interested in visiting a physiotherapist to develop exercise for maintaining joint mobility and spinal flexibility.

The remedy

The first prescription included:

- Valerian to take at night (2 teaspoons tincture)

Her daily mixture consisted of:

- Ginger – circulatory and digestive tonic, carminative
- Vervein – relaxant, bitter tonic
- Passionflower – relaxant
- Meadowsweet – anti-spasmodic, anti-inflammatory.

This remedy improved sleep but she caught a chest infection soon after her first consultation so taking herbal medicine was deferred for two weeks while she took antibiotics. She suffered further weight loss and loose stools but was eating small regular meals. Slippery elm tablets (a soothing antacid) were added to her prescription which was slightly changed to:

- Aniseed – antispasmodic, carminative.
- Vervein – relaxant, bitter tonic.
- Passionflower – relaxant.
- Meadowsweet – anti-spasmodic, anti-inflammatory.

This remedy brought complete relief from all digestive symptoms and lessened the joint pain considerably, although the stiffness didn't entirely disappear. Mrs H continued this medicine on a monthly basis, including her night time mix. She said that she felt less anxious when taking herbal medicine and requested a 'rolling programme' of herbal medicine with the same strategic aims but slight variations on ingredients so that she could continue to benefit on a long-term basis.

Case 5 Mental exhaustion and panic attacks

Miss C, a 42 year old office worker, was caring for her elderly mother in the last stages of a long illness and working full-time in a busy office. She had a teenage family and her husband's work was very insecure. She was feeling permanently exhausted but unable to sleep at night. Her digestive system was erratic, with bouts of constipation followed by diarrhoea in weekly episodes, and constant wind. She was unable to pursue any sports due to the pressures of working and looking after her mother as well as her family. She was experiencing breathlessness, swollen ankles and much lighter menstrual periods. She had recently developed a fear of small spaces, suffering a choking sensation in buses, trains and lifts. Mrs C described herself as being ' at the end of her tether' and wondered whether herbal medicine might help.

The strategy

Mrs C's priority was to obtain relief from anxiety and feelings of panic, to improve digestion and eliminate water retention.

The remedy

- Valerian – relaxant, sedative.
- Borage – adrenal tonic, antidepressant.
- Dandelion leaf – diuretic, bitter tonic.
- Celery seed – diuretic, anti-inflammatory.

Mrs C was also advised to seek further investigation of her heart function as nothing conclusive was revealed on examination. She arranged to have blood tests to check her iron level and thyroid function in order to eliminate all causes of her breathlessness and ankle swelling.

The result

This brought a general improvement in Mrs C's ability to cope, although the pressure on her remained very high. Her panic attacks disappeared completely over three months, although she described a feeling of underlying tension which hadn't gone away, and her sleep remained poor. A night-time mix of valerian and lettuce leaf was added, which gave her two or three full nights' sleep per week. She continued to take herbal medicine for a year, during which her mother died. She described the herbal medicine as a 'life-line' at a very difficult stage in her life. Her hospital investigations showed an iron deficiency but no major problems in her circulatory system. Mrs C began to reduce her herbal medicine by small doses at the end of the year.

Case 6 Anxiety, depression and agoraphobia

Miss T was a 27 year old secretary living alone who had suffered a bout of depression five years before and recently developed a sense of claustrophobia when travelling on the tube. She began to faint in tube trains and described a feeling of 'permanent butterflies' in the stomach. She said that she lost all sensation in her legs and arms when very nervous. She smoked heavily – about twenty cigarettes a day – and relied on alcohol to relax, having brandy at home in the evening and beer at lunch. She had remained mildly depressed since her first major episode for which she had received hospital treatment. She took Prothiaden daily, which didn't appear to help, but she was worried about relapsing if she stopped.

Miss C ate a poor diet, often missing evening meals, and sleeping for most of the time she spent at home.

The strategy

Miss C's priorities were to feel less anxious and recover energy so that she didn't want to sleep all the time. She agreed that her diet could be improved and that this might give her more energy. She planned to reduce smoking slowly and changed from spirits to wine in the evening to change her habit and reduce alcohol intake. She was going to reduce her Prothiaden dose by one third each month.

The remedy

- St John's wort – anti-depressant (increased from 10 to 25ml per week over three months).
- Valerian – relaxant.
- Oats – nervous restorative, tonic.

- Borage – Adrenal tonic, anti-depressant.

The result

This worked extremely well – at the end of the first month she reported changing her job and moved house two months later. Miss T described her overall health as excellent, and continued to take herbal medicine for two more months, reducing the dose in the last month.

Sources and resources

Nutrition – further reading

MAFF Manual of Nutrition (HMSO). A brief guide to the contents of major foods and dietary guidelines with daily requirements. This book was used by every home economics student and teacher from the 1950s until the 1980s when cookery and nutrition became design and labelling!

Identifying herbs – further reading

The Concise British Flora, W. Keble-Martin (Ebury Press). The author was a vicar who spent all his spare time painting wild flowers. This is a remarkable book which captures the essence of each flower and plant. Better than photos for identifying difficult to recognise subjects. Not easy to use, as the plants are arranged in families, but worth persevering.

Exercise

The British Wheel of Yoga, 25 Jermyn St, Sleaford, Lincolnshire NG34 7RU. Tel: (01529) 303233. The main association for yoga teachers and those interested in yoga. Hatha yoga is the type which has most general application – it is yoga for health. This is mainly what you will find being taught in evening classes and lunchtime sessions.It consists of a series of tone and stretch exercises which have been developed over thousands of years in India.

Most teachers include some exercises from other strands of yoga as these are more directly designed to relax the mind and are associated with meditation. Some people with strong religious faiths are afraid that yoga involves taking up a mystic religion. This isn't true – the meditations are designed to make you aware of your mind and enable you to empty it. They can be performed by members of any religious group.

Seeds

King's Seeds, Monk's Farm, Coggeshall Road, Kelvedon, Essex CO5 9PG. Tel (01376) 572456. Previously known as Suffolk Herbs, this is the only company in Britain selling a wide variety of wild flower and herb seeds.

Samuel Dobie and Son, Long Rd, Paignton, Devon TQ4 7SX. Tel (01803) 696444. Dobie's Seeds sells a wide range of flower and vegetable seeds, with a good selection of culinary herbs.

Seeing herbs

The Chelsea Physic Garden, Royal Hospital Walk (entrance in Cheyne Walk), London. Tel: (0207) 352 5646. (Sloane Square tube). Probably the best collection in Britain, begun in the seventeenth century, brilliant teas and cakes, exquisite pleasure to walk round. Open Sundays from 2pm and some weekdays. Run by volunteers (who make the cakes!).

Buying dried herbs and preparations

Alban Mills Herbs, 38 Sandridge Road, St Albans AL1 4AS.
Tel: (01727) 858243. *www.lsgmill@care4free.net*.
A very large range of medicinal and culinary herbs and
spices, creams, oils, syrups, tablets, toiletries and essential
oils. Small amounts no problem.

Gardening

The Henry Doubleday Research Association, Ryton
Gardens, Ryton in Dunsmore, near Coventry. The
Association has it's own seed catalogue, run by Chase
Organics, and a magazine for subscribers which gives
advice on organic gardening and news of organic projects
in Britain and abroad.

Gardener's Question Time, 2pm, Sunday Radio 4, repeated
in the day-time during the week, has been offering
gardening advice from a panel of experts to live audiences
for generations. *Gardener's World*, 8.30 Friday BBC2, offers
half-an-hour of gardening tips.

Consulting herbalists

The National Institute of Medical Herbalists (NIMH), 56
Longbrook St, Exeter, Devon EX4 6AH. Tel: (01392)
426022. *www.btinternet.com/~nimh/*.
Established in 1864 to promote training and standards in
herbal medicine. It is the oldest body of professional
herbalists in the world. Members train for four years to a

BSc in Herbal Medicine, which involves herbal pharmacology, medical sciences and pharmacognosy (the science of recognising herbal compounds and materials).

Representatives of the NIMH sit on government committees and are involved in decisions on the safety of herbal medicines in Britain and Europe.

Counselling and talking therapies

Self help books are abundant, you will need to read more than one to get an idea of the different sorts of talking therapies.

Patient support groups

These are extremely useful for sharing problems and solutions. Ask in your local library for the *Directory of Associations* which contains all national associations and is updated annually.

List of herbs within their applications

Nervous restoratives

Betony
Oats
Skullcap
St John's wort

Relaxants

Black horehound
Catnip
Chamomile
Hops
Kava-kava
Lemon balm
Limeflowers
Passionflower
Verbena
Vervein

Hypnotics

Poppy
Valerian
Wild lettuce

Adaptogens

Borage
Ginseng
Gotu kola

Immuno-stimulants

Echinacea
Siberian ginseng

Tonics

Agrimony
Betony
Damiana
Dandelion
Poplar
Rosemary

General Index